NEEDLEPOINT
ON
A SHOESTRING

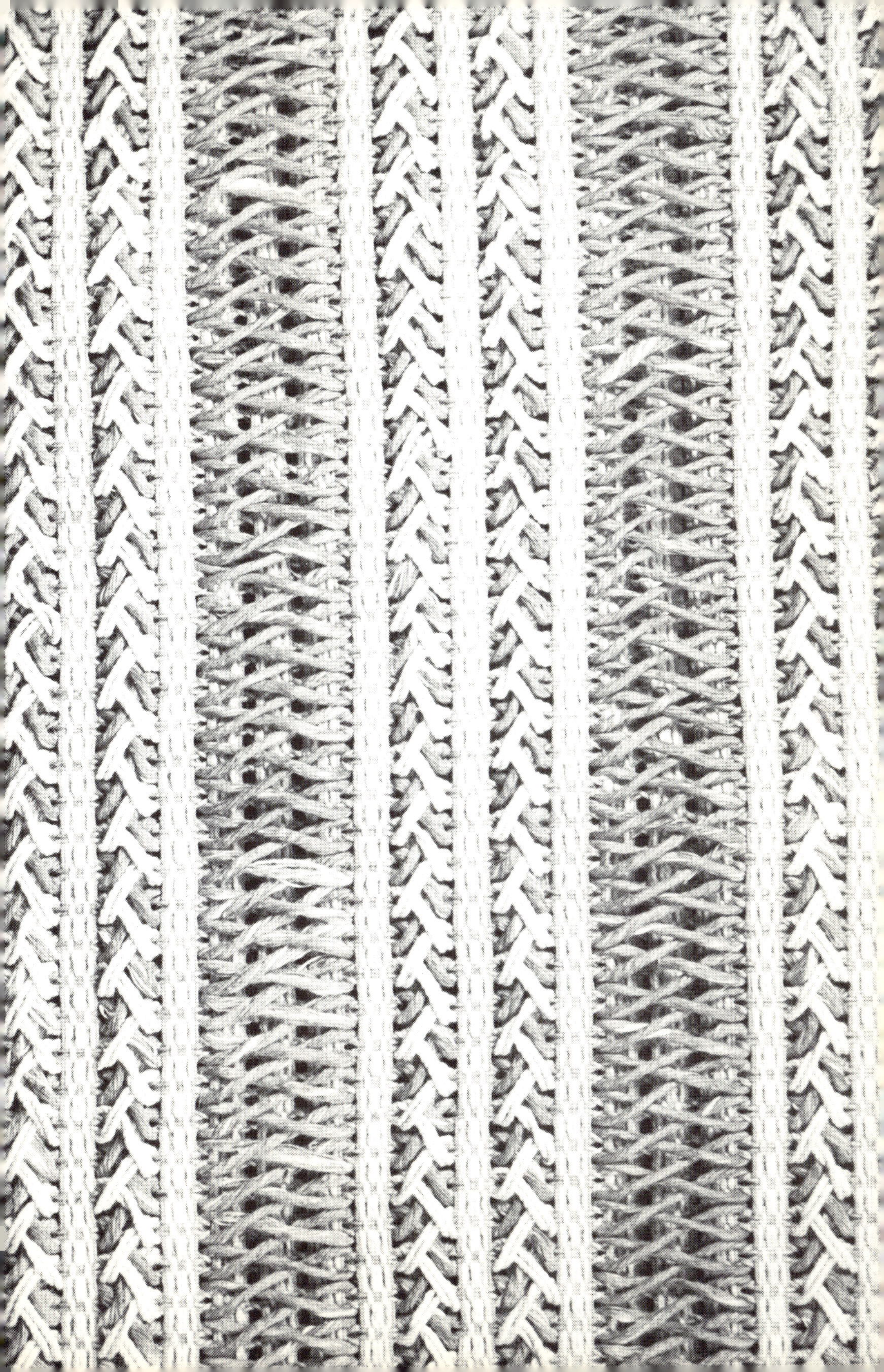

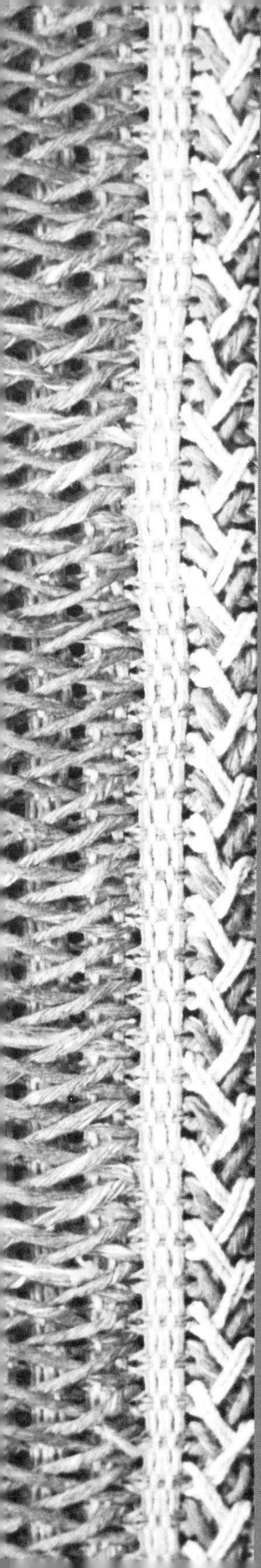

Needlepoint on a Shoestring

Mira Silverstein

Photographs by Salvatore D. Lopes

Diagrams by Roberta Frauwirth

FUNK & WAGNALLS
New York

Published simultaneously in Canada by Fitzhenry & Whiteside Limited, Toronto.

Manufactured in the United States of America

ISBN 0-308-10082-4

1 2 3 4 5 6 7 8 9 10

Library of Congress Cataloging in Publication Data

Silverstein, Mira.
Needlepoint on a shoestring.

1. Canvas embroidery. 2. Embroidery. I. Title.
TT778.C3S55 746.4'4 73-9575
ISBN 0-308-10082-4

To
Dean,
Elise,
Josh,
Shari
and Sal

ACKNOWLEDGMENTS

I wish to thank my dear friend Stella Levy and my daughters Shari and Elise for helping me finish the needlepoint samples in this book.

Contents

An ordinary navy blanket can be changed in an afternoon into a colorful bed cover.

A number of "shoestring" examples and the materials to make them out of, including an embroidered denim jacket, raffia beach bag (hanging on wall), Turkey knot on Rya cloth, butterfly design in heavy Yarn-Tys, Bargello design in Yarn-Tys (at center), handbag of macramé cord (at right) and string on Rya cloth (at front).

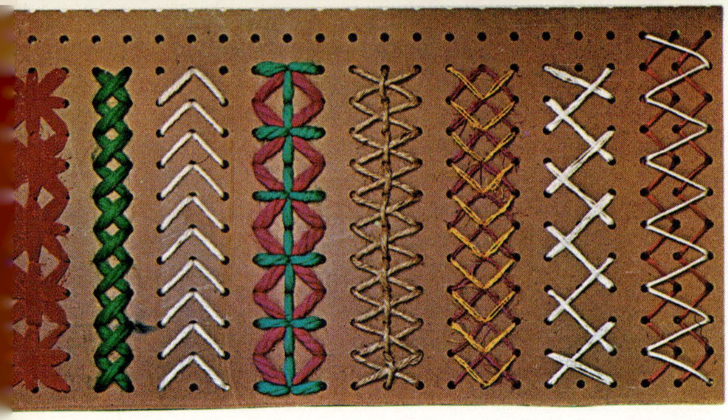

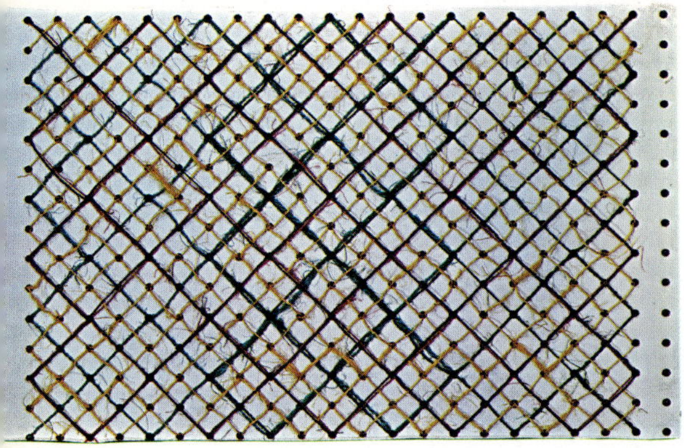

Pegboards, painted or unpainted, can become attractive, informal wall hangings.

Right from top, belts made from macra-cord, sisal, rattail; purse of ribbon worked on Rya cloth; handbag of natural undyed yarns. Center from top, Smyrna Cross pattern in bright yarns; mirror frame of embroidered burlap; piece of overembroidered cloth. Left from top, jute belt; raffia and yarn eyeglass cases.

Introduction

For some time, I have been experimenting with materials other than the standard tapestry yarns and the standard canvas backing for use in needlepoint. As I use the word *needlepoint,* it is a general term for all decorative work done with a threaded needle. Whether it is done on open mesh canvas with a blunt tapestry needle or on a tightly woven fabric with a sharp embroidery needle, it is all needlepoint.

My search for unusual materials has been fascinating and the experiments exciting. In this book, I would like to share with you some of the results of my needlepointing on a shoestring.

Most of the materials used in this book are inexpensive and readily available. When materials are more costly, they are used with economy so that a comparatively large project may be finished, literally, on a shoestring.

Although I have given some specific patterns, this is not primarily a book of patterns. They are trendy and fashion changes constantly. Use the ideas and the stitch patterns to make your own designs. Experiment with other media and see what you come up with.

Everything was tested for reasonable durability. Bear in mind, however, that needlepoint on a shoestring is mostly fun. The projects are easy to do and quick to finish. The cost is negligible. Don't place an heirloom value on everything. Enjoy it for as long as it gives you pleasure, then discard it and make a new one.

MATERIALS

String

String is one of the most versatile media for use in craft projects. It comes in a large selection of weights and degrees of pliability, and, when testing it for needlepoint, I found the results most interesting.

Ordinary wrapping string is very inexpensive and is sold in stationery, hardware, and five-and-ten-cent stores. The color range is mostly white or oatmeal for cotton and nylon string and wheat brown for jute. Sometimes, a lovely twisted mason line is available in pale yellow as well as white. This is an even-textured, durable string of excellent quality that does not shed and is highly recommended for outdoor furniture covers.

Sisal twine is rather coarse, "hairy" and loosely twisted. It is the color of pale straw and comes in several weights. Sisal twine has an interesting texture when worked with bulky stitches on wide mesh canvas.

Jute is a very pliable wheat brown string available in a number of weights. It is quite inexpensive when purchased in hardware stores. Jute cord is also sold in craft shops for use in macramé. It is considerably more expensive but it comes in a variety of lovely colors.

Jute tends to shed somewhat when drawn through canvas. Bear this in mind before settling down in a velvet upholstered chair with jute needlework. The end result, however, is lovely and the shedding does stop. The belt and handbag on page 77 are worked with jute cord in wheat brown. The director's chair on page 64 was worked with the navy jute cord used in macramé.

There is a multi-ply cotton string that looks like jute at first glance. The brown dye coats the thin strands and makes them stick together as one for extra strength. This string is rather inflexible when new, but after working with it on needlepoint canvas, it softens. The threads separate slightly and show up white in the center. The effect is most charming. This is the most commonly available string and the least expensive. Unfortunately, it is sold unmarked. Twist a small piece between your fingers to test it. If the thin strands separate and show a lighter color within, then you have the right one.

Since commercial string is obviously not intended for needlepoint, very little is known about its properties other than strength. If you want to use it for needlepoint, you must test it first. Thread it through a needle (it is wise to have several types handy), work it on a canvas backing, try several of the stitches suggested on page 17 and examine the effect.

String is not as soft nor as pliable as wool yarn. It should be worked on a larger mesh canvas with bulky stitches that allow the canvas to show through. Canvas has an interesting texture of its own that may be incorporated into the total design. When working with string, avoid using the slanted needlepoint stitches such as Continental, Scotch or Cash-

mere. These tend to distort the canvas and the work will require blocking, but blocking is not recommended for string needlework.

Another source of string for needlework is the gift wrapping counter in most department stores and card shops. Brightly colored string may be purchased in small packages. This string is somewhat uneven in texture but great fun to work with.

Colored string is not always colorfast and should be tested before it is used for needlework. It does not have to be washable, but you don't want it rubbing off on everything it touches. Hold it in your hand for a few minutes. If it leaves a stain, don't use it.

Ordinary string can be tinted very easily. For cotton and jute, use Tintex dye or Rit dye and follow directions on the package for tinting cotton. Pretest a small amount of string to determine the length of time it takes for it to absorb the desired shade. Unwind the ball of string and shape it into a skein by winding it around a heavy cardboard about 18 inches long. Tie the skein at one end with a piece of string, remove from cardboard, and tint. Rinse thoroughly and hang up to dry. Cut skein at the point where it was tied because that spot will not absorb the color and would show a light spot in your needlework.

On the other hand, if you like a dappled or tie-dyed look, cut the string in equal lengths (whatever length you find comfortable to work with). Tie several strands together with tight knots placed at 4- or 5-inch intervals. Repeat with the rest of the string and tint, again following directions on the package. Dry thoroughly before untying knots. (On page 19 is an example of tie-dyed string worked in the Smyrna Cross stitch on canvas.)

When dying yarn or string, be sure to dye all you need for a given project at one time.

Macramé Supplies

Macramé supply houses offer a wealth of unusual materials that may be worked with a needle. These are more expensive than commercial twine but they are sold as craft media and are therefore more consistent in texture and quality. They also come in a large variety of colors.

Macramé materials used in this book are only a small cross section of the unlimited range of textures and colors available in this field. I used the following: navy cord, a fine but very strong and pliable polished string, which comes in several good colors as well as black and white; rattail, a smooth, shiny, rather heavy rayon cord in beautiful bright colors, which looks striking worked in the Herringbone stitch on #3½ canvas; macra-cord, a heavy, slightly textured synthetic cord that works up much the same as rattail but is not as shiny; and linen rug warp, an elegant string made of natural linen thread. It does not come in colors. Weavers use it as rug warp, but it lends itself beautifully to needlepoint. The window shade (page 70) and the bag and belt set (page 77) were made with it.

Ribbons

Using ribbon for needlepoint is not original. Our grandmothers used a thin silky ribbon over a soft open mesh to create fragile doilies that are perhaps collector's items today. Ribbon is colorful and fun to use. The crinkling and puckering that is formed as it is pulled through the canvas mesh creates an interesting texture. You can make some very attractive handbags, belts and wall hangings with ribbon needlepoint.

Ribbon is not inexpensive but a little goes a long way, for the stitches are wide and need spacing. Save leftover ribbon, watch for special sales and use sparingly. There is an interesting gadget called a fabric slitter that is commonly used for making rag rugs. It clamps onto the edge of a table and a small crank handle operates a sharp cutting wheel. This wheel will cut fabric into strips of varying widths that may be used as ribbons for needlepoint. Use fabric with a dense weave and a low pile. Test the first few strips for strength and degree of fraying. A little fraying lends some interest to the overall texture, but too much fraying is not only messy but tends to weaken the fabric.

Raffia made of polypropylene is washable, nonfading, extremely pliable and very inexpensive. It comes in a selection of lovely colors and works up into beautiful summer accessories such as beach bags, sunglass cases and as overembroidery on beach hats and sandals.

Yarns

If you purchase undyed wool yarns and use them in their natural shades or learn to dye them yourself, you can save up to 50% of the cost of a needlework project. Heavy rug yarn may be used in combination with macramé cord for most unusual textures on handbags or belts.

Dyeing wool yarns is a very simple matter. A small amount of special wool dye, available commercially, is mixed in very hot water in a glass or enamel pan. The dry yarn is dipped into this dye solution, swished around a bit and allowed to soak until it acquires the proper shade. The yarn is then removed, soaked in some fresh hot water, cooled, drained and dried. There is no "cooking" and no need for special additives if you use acidified yarns.

An interesting "shoestring" yarn is a very heavy wool called "Yarn-Tys," which is sold in small packages at gift-wrapping counters and is available in a very large selection of colors. There is a single weight that will cover the widest canvas mesh and there is also a double weight that produces enormous Cross stitches like the ones shown in the picture on the jacket of this book.

Acrylic yarns that are machine washable and cotton embroidery floss come in many beautiful colorfast shades and are perfect for decorative embroidery on machine-washable fabrics.

Shoelaces and Others

Shoelaces are fun to work with, but are too expensive for large projects. Old ones, however, are good craft projects for youngsters. Save those that have at least one tip left. Wash thoroughly, dry and work through canvas mesh using the tip as the "needle." Cotton shoelaces may be tinted.

Costlier materials used in small amounts can go a long way to create something pretty and inexpensive. The denim jacket on page 83 was embroidered with a few strands of bright persian yarns and a few sequins. Two or three strands of tapestry yarn or silk thread embroidered on the collar and cuffs of a simple shirt or blouse is decorative. Be sure to use colorfast threads on washable fabrics.

Canvas

The most commonly used backing for needlepoint, this is a heavily sized cotton fabric with an even weave and open mesh. It is identified by the number of mesh squares per linear inch. For example, #5 canvas has five squares to the inch. The heaviest canvas available to date is #3½.

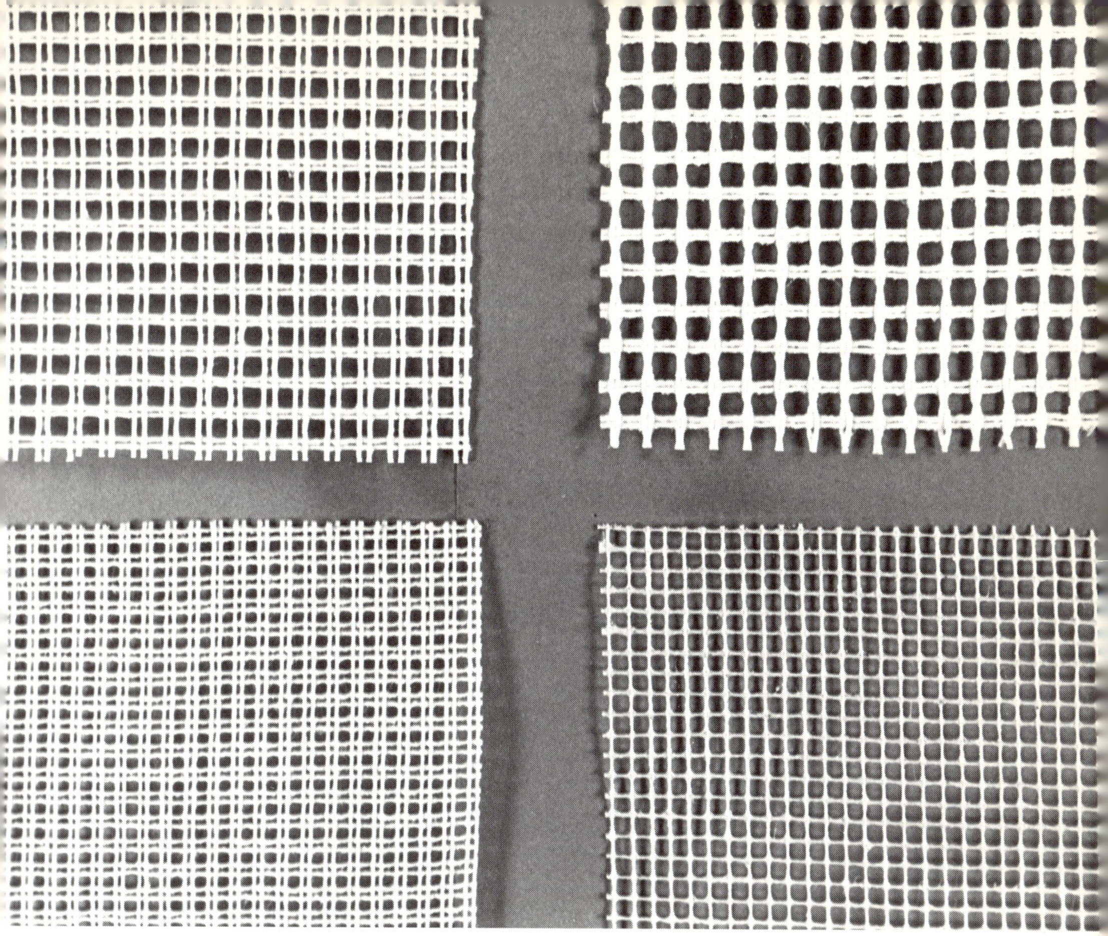

Four types of canvas suitable for string needlework. Top left, #4 double mesh; top right, #3½ Lino canvas (twisted double mesh). Bottom left, #5 double mesh; bottom right, #6 single mesh.

For string and bulky yarns, use the heaviest canvas because it offers a firm backing. Canvas also comes in a lighter gauge which is not recommended for string work. I use it in making belts, pockets, buttons, eyeglass cases and other lightweight articles worked with tapestry yarn or cotton thread. The handbag and belt set on page 77 and the window shade on page 70 were worked with linen rug warp on a 6-inch single mesh canvas. You will notice that in all the needle-

point articles worked with string, the canvas is allowed to show through. The finished design is more textured and, of course, it takes less time to finish. Canvas may be tinted with indelible markers or a thin solution of artist's oil paints or acrylics. It should be tinted before it is worked with yarn or string and allowed to dry thoroughly. Don't dip canvas into a hot dye solution because it will soften the sizing in the canvas. String work requires a very firm backing.

In addition to canvas, there are several softer fabrics that are strong enough to use even as carpet backing. They have a lovely texture, an open weave and are fun to use for needlepoint with soft bulky yarns.

Monk's Cloth

A very soft two-ply sturdy cotton fabric in widths up to 186 inches. A good even weave, it is excellent for Cross stitches as well as for free-form stitchery. It may be used for tablecloths, coverlets and other larger projects as well as for handbags and pillows.

Knot-On

This is a very heavy single-ply cotton fabric with an unusual silky texture. The wide open mesh accommodates the heaviest yarns and needles. It is not suitable for string.

Dura-Back

Very much like Knot-on but a little lighter in weight, Dura-back lends itself beautifully to decorative embroidery with medium or heavy yarns. Both fabrics are available in 72-inch

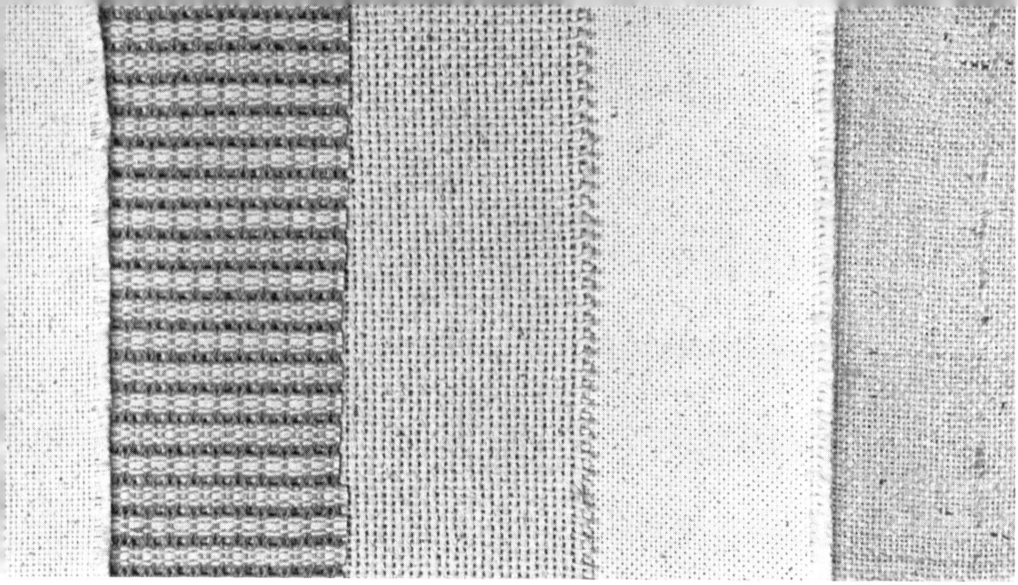

Various kinds of backings. Left to right: Monk's cloth, Rya cloth, Knot-on, Dura-back and burlap.

widths. Both are unfamiliar to the needlepoint public, since they are used mainly for hooked rugs. However, their texture is so lovely that I often use them in making embroidered coverlets, drapes, pillow tops or large handbags.

Like all cotton fabrics, these are easily tinted with household tints such as Rit dye and Tintex dye. Follow manufacturer's directions for tinting cotton. Pretest a small sample. A heavier fabric may take a little longer to absorb dye. Bear in mind, too, that most of these fabrics are not preshrunk, and will tighten a little after being soaked in hot water or dye solution. If that happens, some of the effects may prove quite interesting. I suggest that you fold over and machine stitch the edges of these fabrics before working with them. A loosely woven fabric will ravel very quickly, especially when dipped in water. Tape will soften when wet and fall away.

Burlap

A very popular fabric, fun to use, in natural wheat or bright colors. Very good background for simple stitchery. The nat-

ural burlap may be tinted, but it will take on a darker hue. Burlap texture may be altered slightly by soaking it in very warm water for a few minutes. The normally flat fibers shrink a little, becoming rounder and separating slightly from each other. The effect is almost that of coarse linen and quite attractive. Smooth the soaking wet burlap with your hands on a flat surface and let dry. This eliminates the need for ironing. Burlap must be edged with a machine-stitched seam to prevent raveling.

Rya Cloth

A familiar rug backing with alternating lines of tightly woven cloth and evenly spaced openings. It is used mainly for working looped stitches that are cut to make shag or rya rugs. This cloth has a beautiful weave that may be incorporated as part of the overall design and can be worked with a number of large stitches.

Other Fabrics

Virtually any fabric that is used for clothing, accessories or upholstery may be decorated with needlepoint. Linen, cotton, silk and some synthetic fabrics may be overembroidered in a variety of ways. First, test the fabric to see if it is easily pierced with a needle. The needle may have to be heavy or thin, long or short, but it should slide easily through the fabric. Unlike string, which may require some tugging, soft yarns used for embroidery should be handled gently. A tightly woven fabric such as duck or Indian Head may be very difficult to embroider. New, heavy-duty denim may have to be softened with several washings before it can be worked with an embroidery needle. You will find that laminated, rubberized and bonded

fabrics are unsuitable for needlework. Test a small area of a selected fabric to see for yourself.

If you have a fabric in a solid color and a smooth surface, trace a pattern on it and embroider it with suitable yarns using one of the recommended stitches on pages 40–45. Printed fabrics may be overembroidered by outlining the entire printed pattern or only part of it with matching yarns.

Inexpensive blankets, the type sold in army and navy surplus or camping supply stores, are excellent shoestring needlepoint projects. Use a free-form design of your own choosing or trace the one on page 87.

Perforated Metal, Plastic or Wood Pegboard

These make interesting backings for string, cord and heavy yarn. All are available in building supply stores. Any type of wire screening or mesh or even chicken wire will also make an interesting background for heavy string needlework. Work string or yarn in even or random stitches. Use a needle whenever possible. If string is too heavy to thread through a needle, wrap some cellophane tape around the end of the string for about an inch or so. Use it as a needle, and when it begins to fall apart, cut it away and make another tip.

When working with string on a rigid surface, do not use knots or other ordinary methods of fastening yarn. Instead, leave a 3-inch piece at the beginning and at the end of the strand. After completing a few lines, turn the work over and tie the nearest tail ends to each other. Tie them two by two even if they are an inch or so apart. Tie into firm double knots and clip the ends. Make sure that the stitchery on the face of the work conceals the knots on the back. If you want to paint the pegboard, do it before stitching. Use a flat quick-drying paint, cover the surface evenly and be careful not to get paint into the holes.

Various stitches worked on a perforated metal sheet in string, macramé navy cord and thin florist wire (top row).

White rattail macramé cord worked in large Herring-bone stitch on a white plastic fretwork. Open fretwork is visible at the top. Framed in simple white plastic, it makes an attractive wall hanging.

Needles and Other Materials

Needles are very important. Select several sizes with medium and large eyes and keep a good supply on hand. You will need blunt point needles for canvas and other rigid backings with large mesh openings. For fabrics with a tighter weave, use crewel needles. These have sharp points, but the eyes are large enough to accommodate the heavier yarns. Most needlepoint supply stores carry a selection of needles. If you plan to work with beads, be sure to have at least one or two needles that will slide easily through the bead you'll be working with.

Additional materials needed for needlepoint on a shoestring are straight pins, push pins, pencils, pens, transfer paper, a ruler and perhaps a transfer pencil which turns any design into a hot iron transfer.

STITCHES

Needlepoint stitches worked with string should be large and open. I recommend only a few versatile ones which can be used on the small-gauge canvases as well as on the large heavy ones. You will find that the same stitches work well on metal and wood backing.

Cross stitch begins as a half cross worked in one direction to the end of the line. Then the second half is crossed over the first line in the opposite direction. Crosses may be worked one at a time if desired. It is important that all the top lines (second half) face in the same direction.

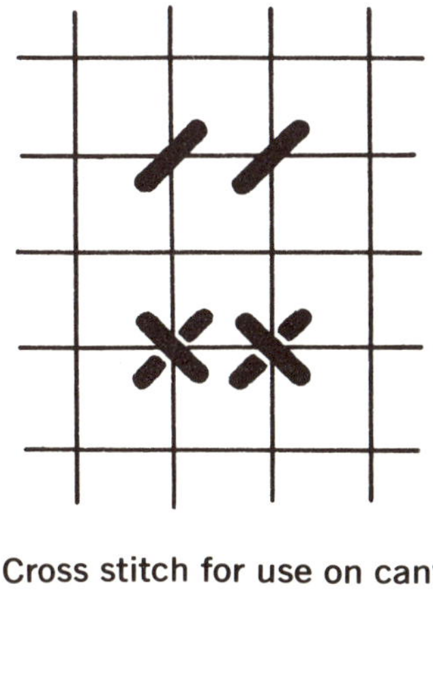

Cross stitch for use on canvas

Cross stitch for use on plain fabric

Double Cross stitch or Smyrna Cross looks like two crosses that overlap. Work the first one with a vertical and then a horizontal line. The last stitch must face in the same direction over the entire work for a nice uniform effect. The Smyrna Cross is worked over a larger area and results in a fuller, bulkier stitch. The second diagram is a variation on the original and is more elongated. Work Smyrna Crosses with a soft, even tension. This makes an interesting design if the background is left unfinished. It can then be filled in with another color or tinted. Tinting must be done before stitching and special care should be taken to dry the paint. If there is a doubt about the indelible quality of the paint, a light spray with a fixative such as Krylon is highly recommended.

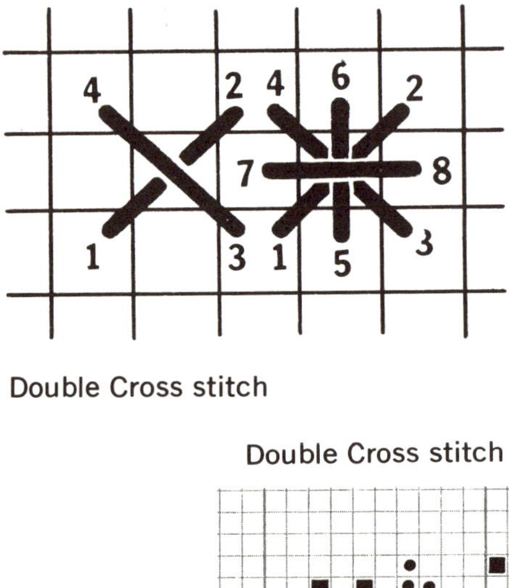

Double Cross stitch

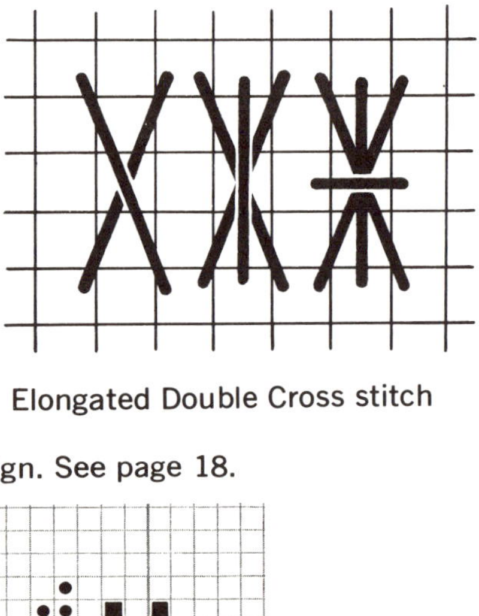

Elongated Double Cross stitch

Double Cross stitch design. See page 18.

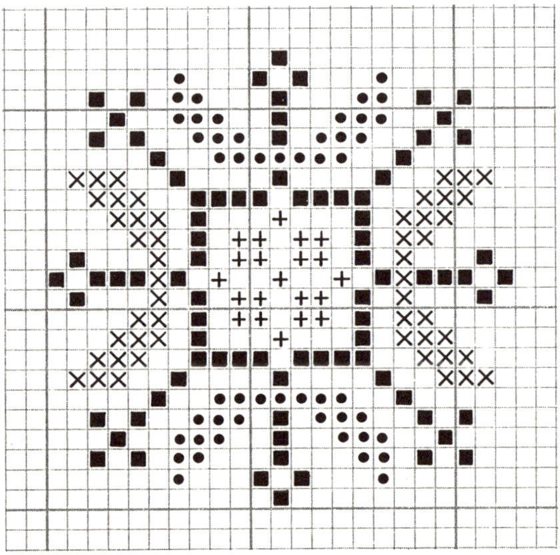

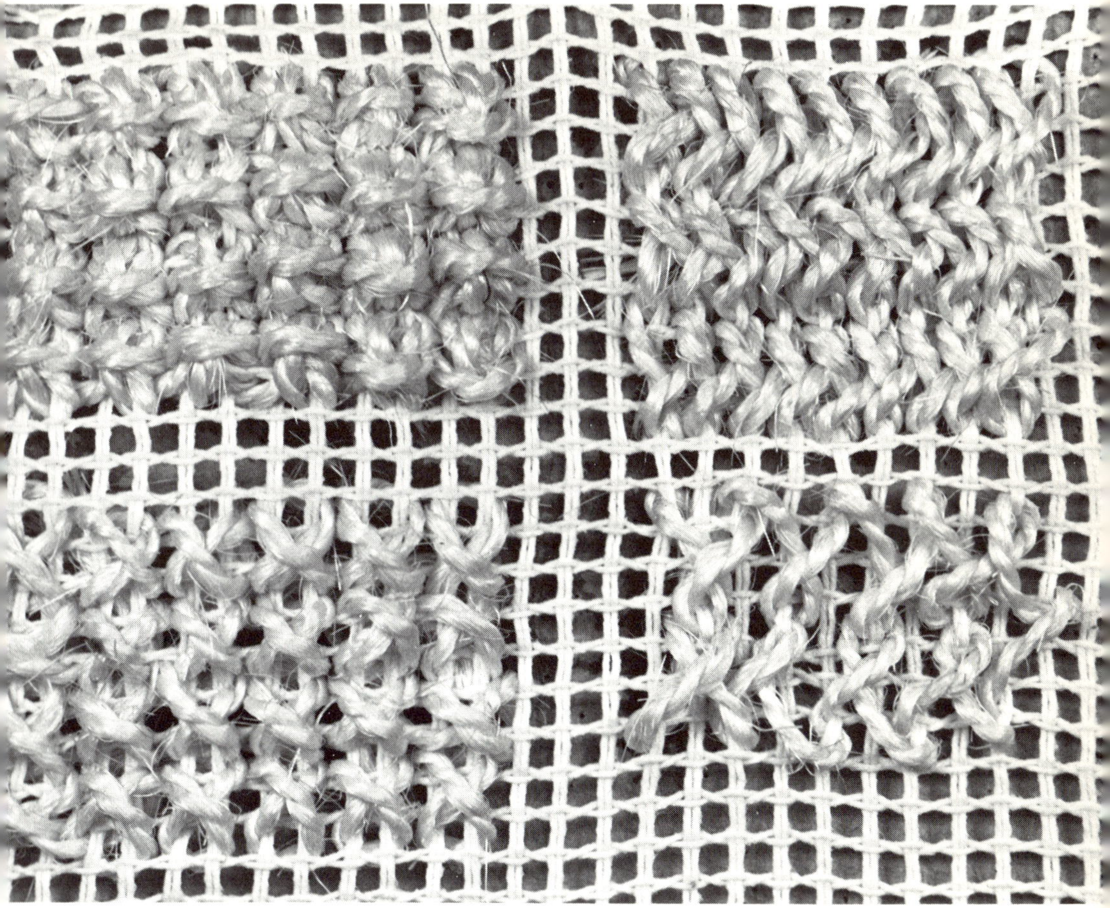

Cross stitch and Herringbone worked in heavy sisal string. These are only samples and indicate the bulky quality of this medium. Don't crowd stitches, work on large mesh canvas, and make large articles such as tote bags, small rugs, etc.

A geometric design in bright tapestry yarns worked in the Smyrna Cross stitch on #4 canvas (also shown in color).

Smyrna Cross stitch in tie-dyed cotton cord on #3½ canvas.

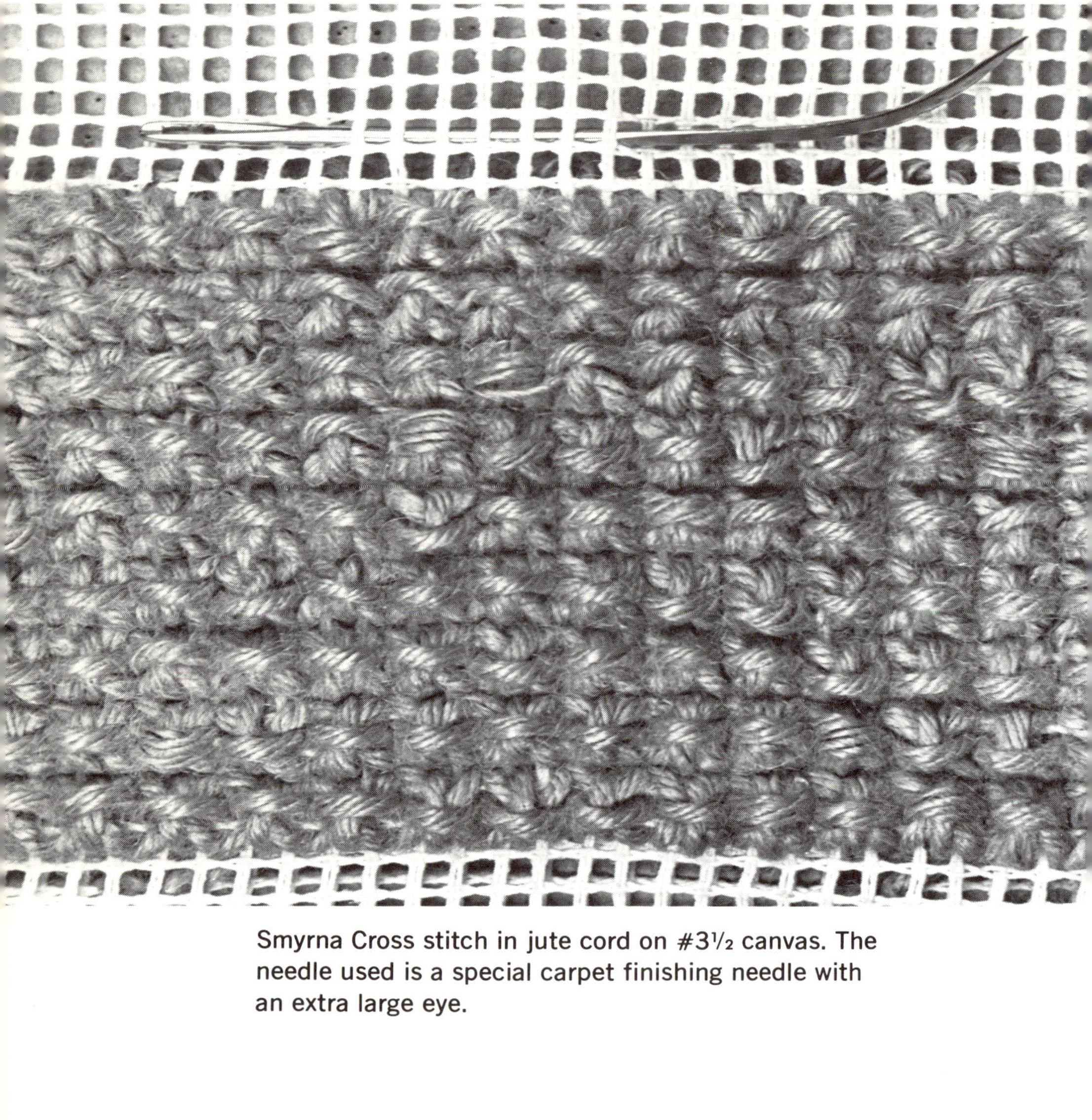

Smyrna Cross stitch in jute cord on #3½ canvas. The needle used is a special carpet finishing needle with an extra large eye.

Herringbone is one of the most versatile needlepoint stitches. It may be used on any fabric as an edging or as part of a design but is especially interesting when worked in two or more colors on canvas. Work from left to right. Take up a strand of canvas at upper left, bring the yarn in a diagonal line to lower right, pick up a strand of canvas in a right to left motion and carry over the thread to the upper right. Continue in this manner and you will find the thread forms a tiny cross at the top and bottom of the line. Study the diagram and practice the stitch. First work the closed herringbone by taking up every strand of canvas at the top and at the bottom of the line. Afterwards, skip a line of canvas between stitches at top and bottom, then skip two lines of canvas, then three and so on. As the herringbone becomes wider, the stitches become longer. Place additional colors into the spaces you skipped. Work the line of stitches the same way, each color separately from left to right. When one line is finished, begin the second line also from left to right but work it in reverse or upside down so that the "Vs" meet end to end. If you study the photographs, you will see several possibilities of color and texture combinations.

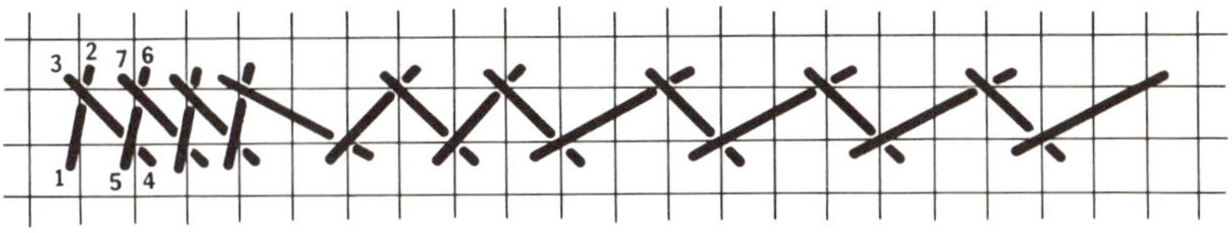

Herringbone stitch as used on canvas

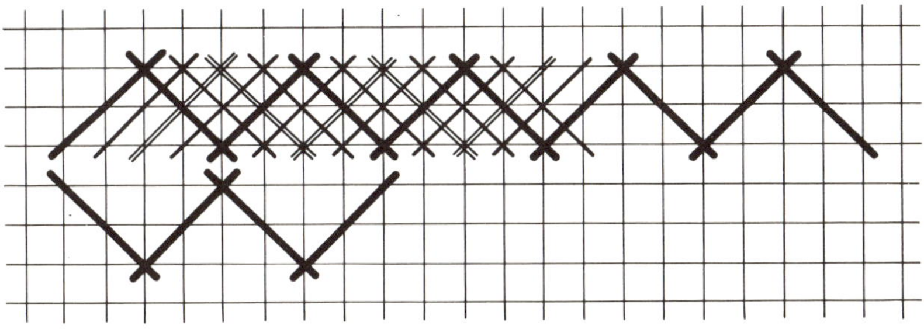

Rya cloth backing worked with Herringbone in alternating long and short stitches.

Rya cloth with a variety of stitches. From top, Short Herringbone, Long Herringbone, Turkey Knot, Cross stitch, Smyrna Cross, Cross stitch and a line, two rows of Herringbone. The first three rows were worked with string, the next three with unbleached wool yarn, and the last with wool yarn and rayon rattail macramé cord.

Herringbone stitch in red and white rattail (also shown in color).

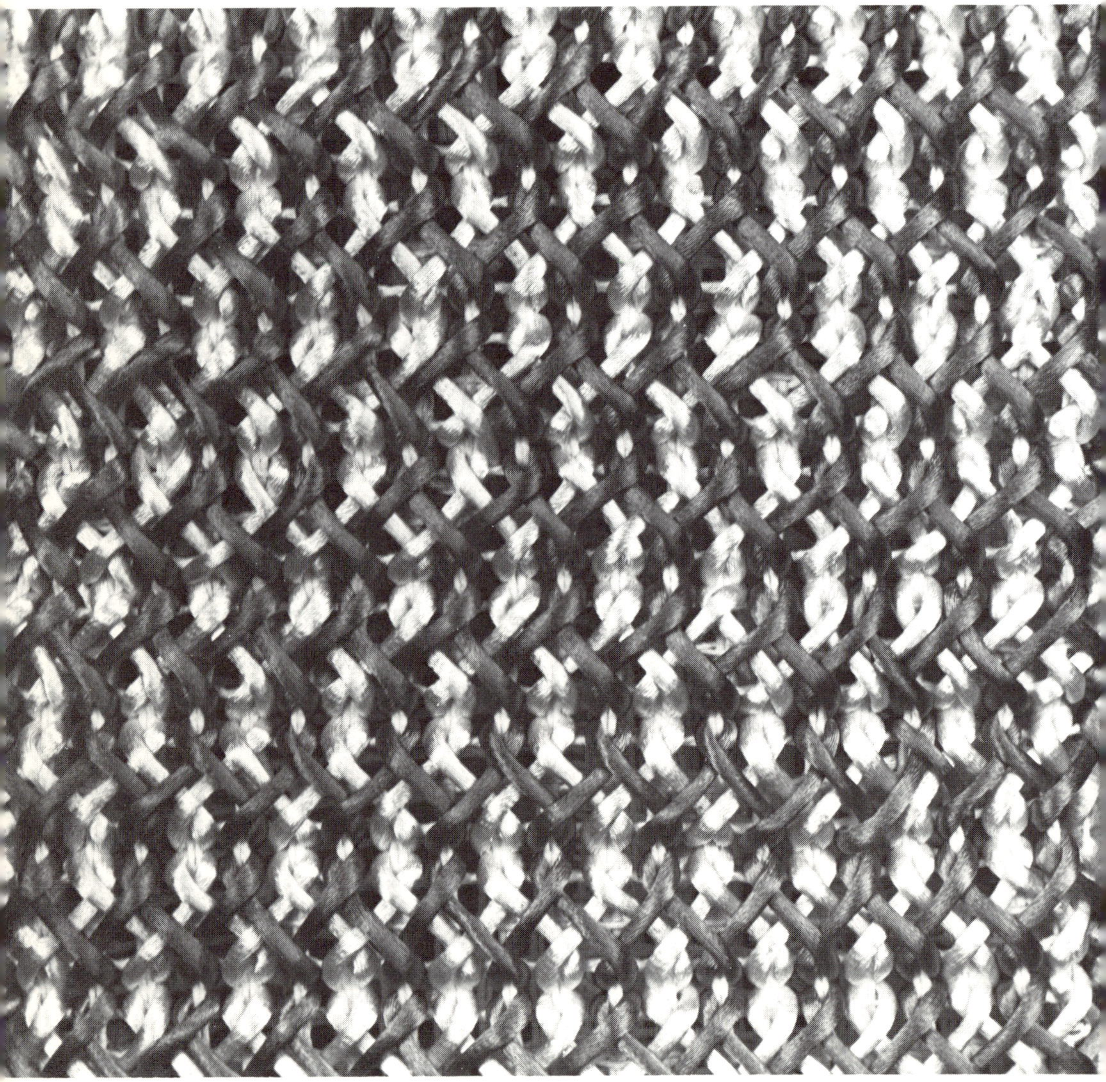

Herringbone stitch in four colors shown in a beach bag worked in raffia (also shown in color).

Turkey Knot is anchored by a little Cross stitch in reverse. Work from left to right in horizontal lines. Look at the diagram and study the numbers. The needle comes in at 1 and out at 2, over to the right at 3 and under to upper left to 4. Now leave a loop as large as you wish, come over and down to the *right* of the previous stitch and repeat. If you look on the reverse side, you will see a tiny cross which anchors the loop and prevents it from slipping. Turkey knots are worked on the right side of the fabric only. When you reach the end of the line, cut the strand of yarn and begin the next row again from left to right. Loops may be worked as long or as short as desired. Cut the tops of the loops for a shag look. Try working this with tie-dyed yarns. Also nice for making fringes.

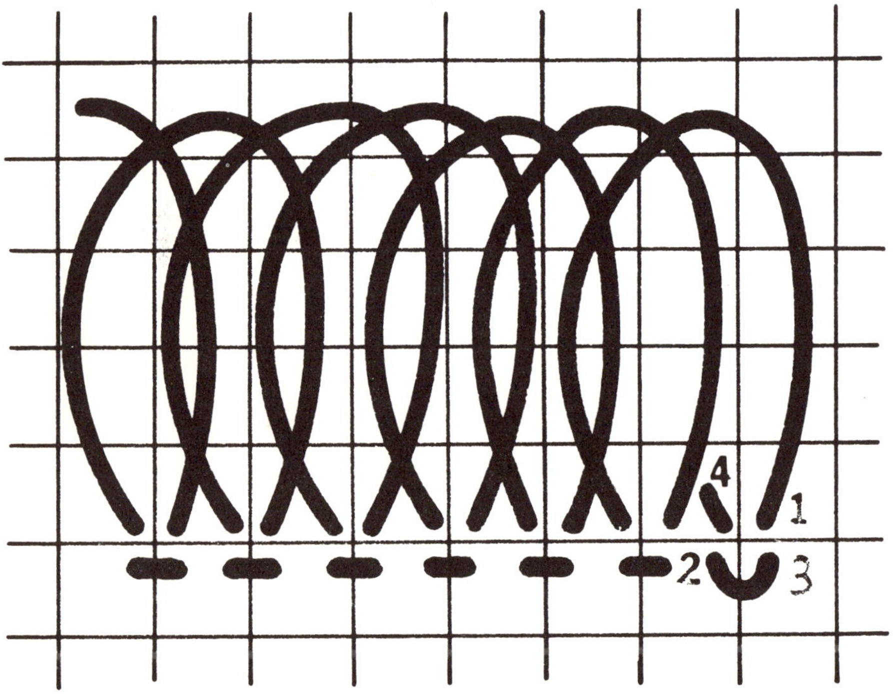

Turkey Knot on Rya cloth worked with tie-dyed wool yarn. The loops were cut short so that part of the cloth would show through. This may be used as a handbag or pillow top (also shown in color).

Chevron is very simple. Work in vertical fashion with half cross stitches going upward. Cross over at the end of the line picking up once again as many strands of canvas and work the half cross in reverse coming downward. Stitches may be large or small, wide or narrow and a row or two of canvas may be skipped between the double rows of chevron. For added interest, canvas may be tinted.

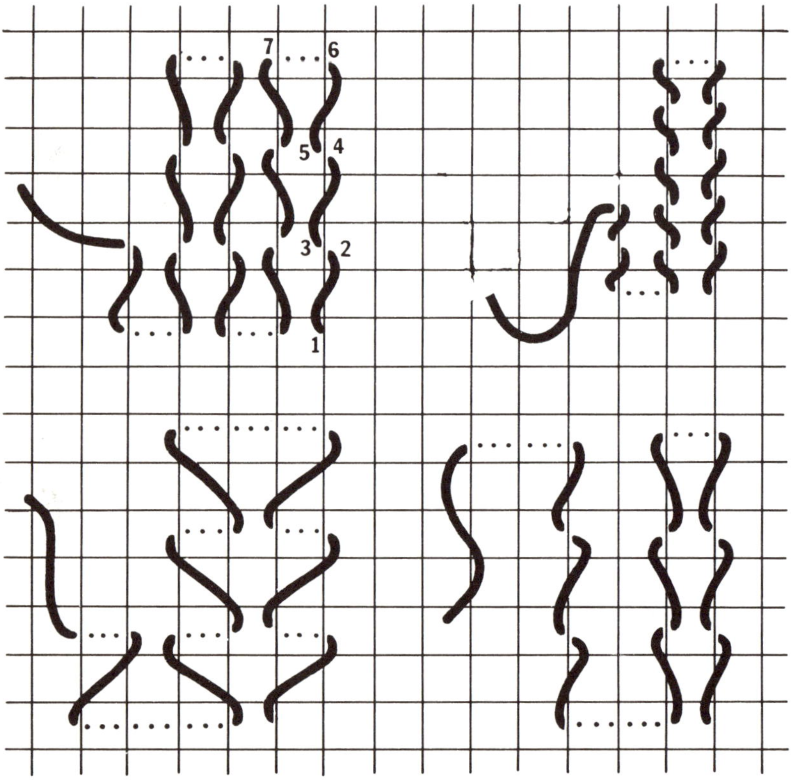

Chevron stitch (upper left) and three variations: narrow (top right), wide (bottom left) and with a row or two of canvas skipped between the double rows (bottom right).

Sample of needlework using shoelaces in Chevron stitch on #3½ canvas. Very good for belts and handbags.

Bargello is a vertical stitch worked over a given number of strands of canvas. It covers a large area very quickly especially when the yarn is thick. Normally Bargello is worked over four strands of canvas, under 2, over 4, under 2, and repeated until the end of the line. All subsequent lines follow the lead or first line. Stitches may be longer if the yarn is heavier. If the yarn is extra heavy, it is simpler to work a brick stitch Bargello by placing a vertical line in every other row of canvas and filling the skipped stitches with a second row of vertical lines, placing them at the half mark. The overall effect is that of interlocking bricks. Study the diagram and practice the stitch.

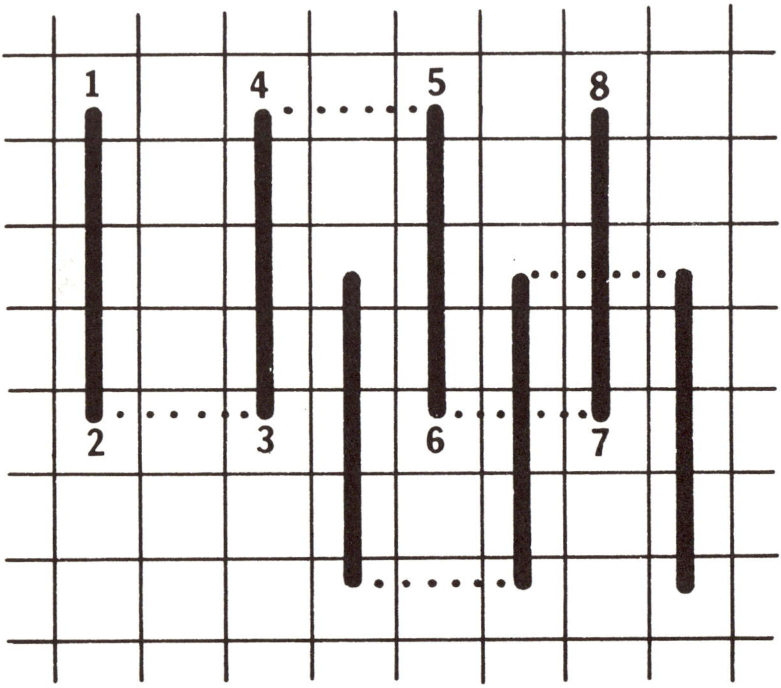

Heavy Yarn-Tys (wool yarn used for gift wrapping) in bright Mexican colors worked in Bargello brick stitch on #3½ canvas (also shown in color).

Open Diamond is very easy and works up very fast. Work from left to right one stitch at a time. Following the first diagram for the regular Open Diamond stitch, begin at 1, carry yarn over diagonally to the left at 2, then under to 3, over to 4, under to 5 and repeat. It looks almost like the Herringbone except that it does not have the tiny crosses at the base of each stitch. When the line is finished, begin at left again but reverse the stitch forming the open diamond. Illustrated are four variations of this stitch. You will notice that the Open Diamond outlines the squares of canvas creating a light, airy design.

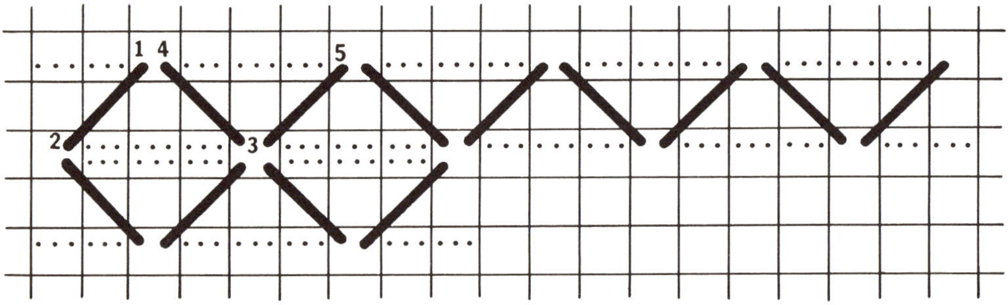

Open Diamond stitch

On pages 33–36 are shown four variations of Open Diamond stitch worked with twisted Mason line on #5 double mesh canvas.

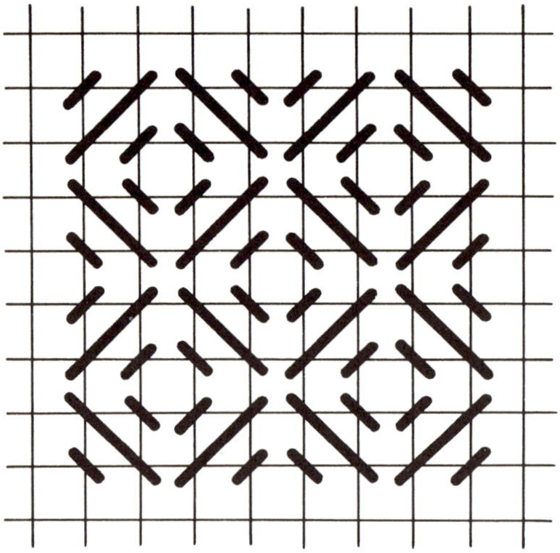

STITCHES

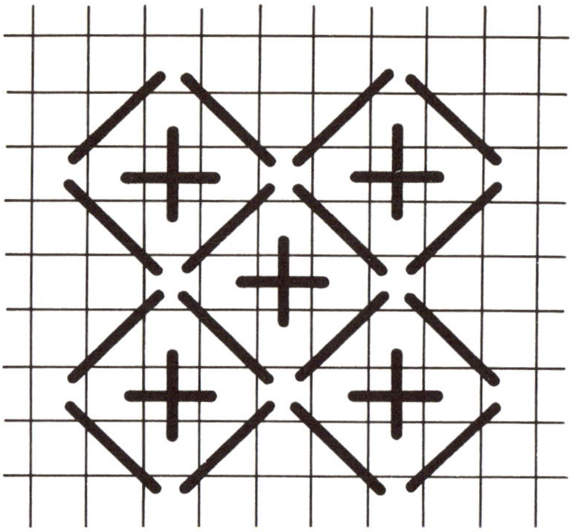

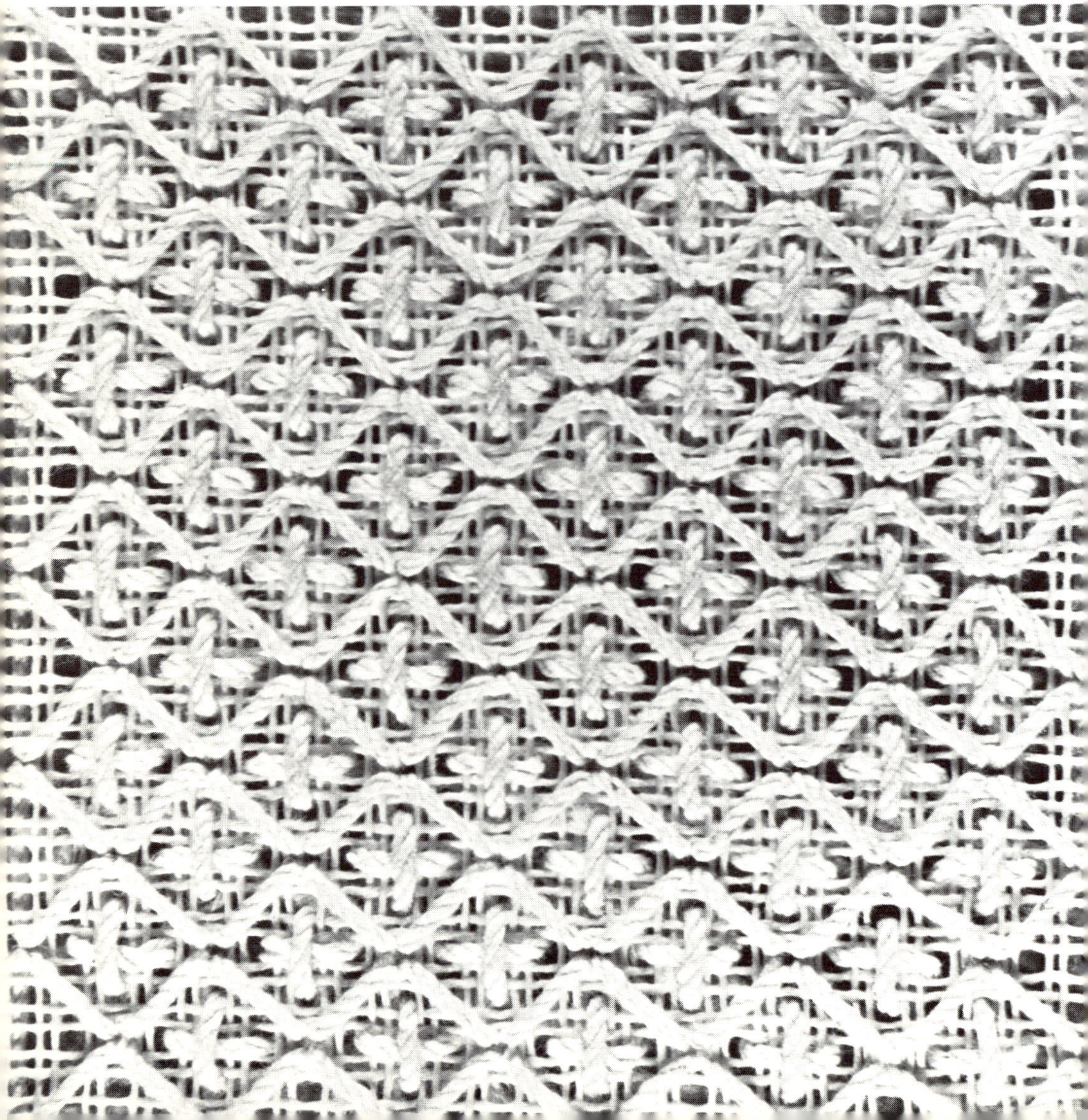

Open Diamond variation with multicolor French Knots
in wool yarn.

Open Diamond in two shades of double weight Yarn-Tys on #3½ canvas. The diamonds crisscross each other and could be finished with large Donkey beads.

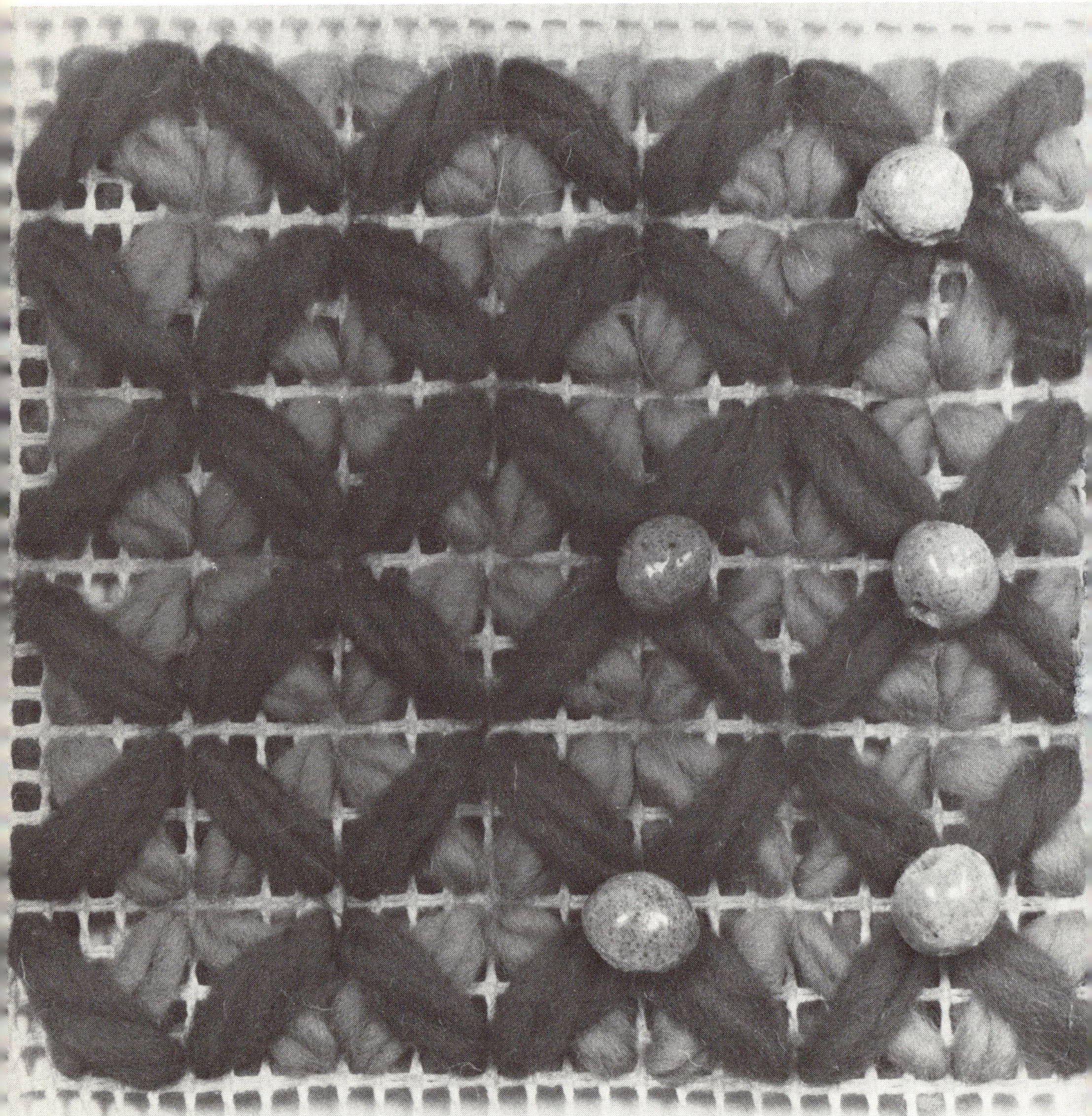

An interesting way to use three different textures in a simple Open Diamond stitch design. The first layer is inexpensive brown string. The second layer, crossing over the first, is shiny rattail. The third, seen in one row at the top, is a textured macra-cord. The string is brown, the rattail is pink and the macra-cord is navy.

STITCHES

There are several good embroidery stitches which can be easily used on fabric other than canvas.

Running stitch is the simplest of all. Work right to left and make stitches as even as possible.

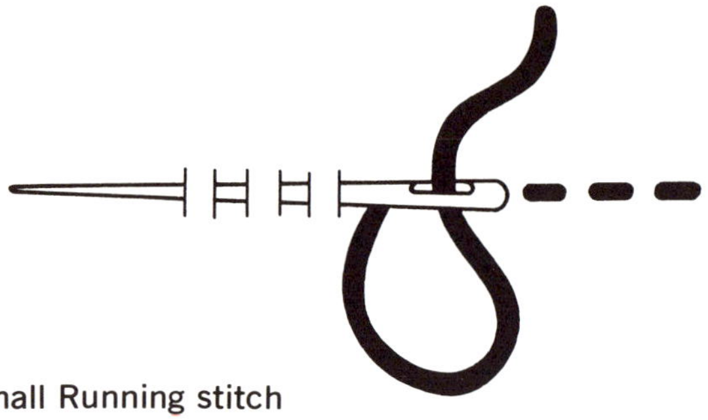

Small Running stitch

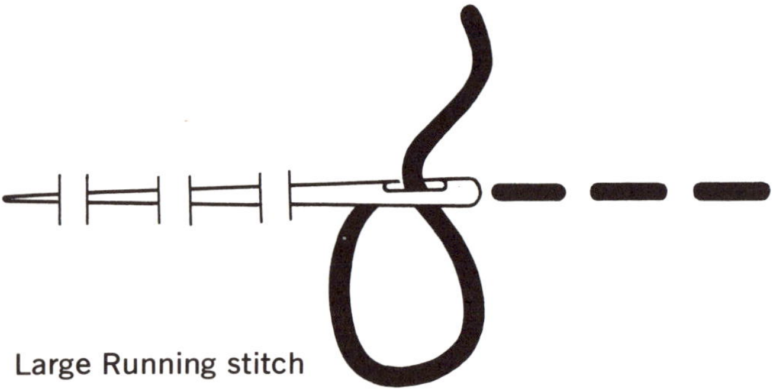

Large Running stitch

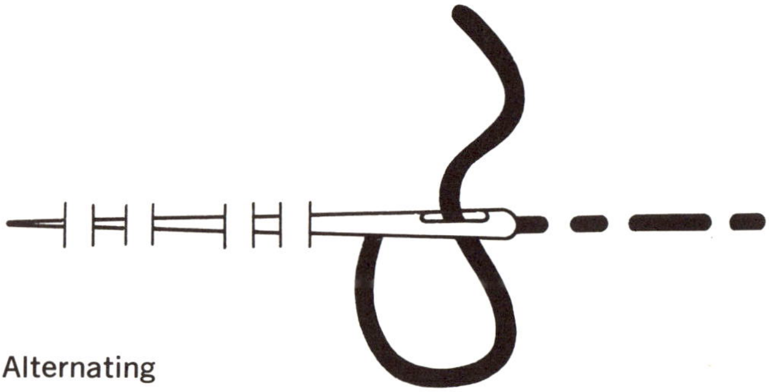

Alternating
Running stitch

Stem stitch is an excellent outline stitch. Work from left to right. Practice by doing straight lines and curves, and keep stitches small and even. Stem stitch may be used to fill in an open area.

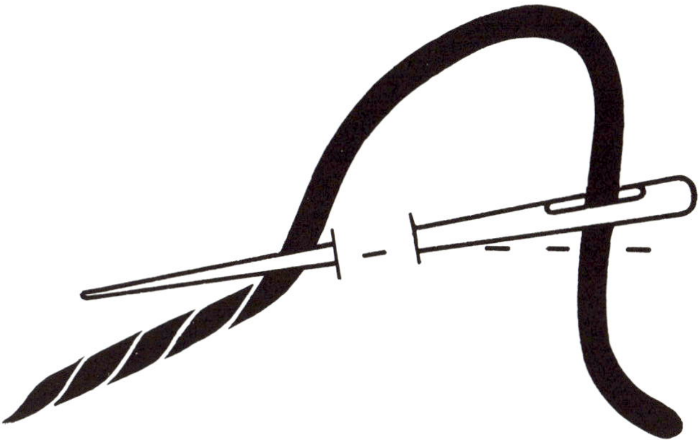

Stem stitch

Stem stitch used as a filling

Chain stitch can be used as an outline or to fill in designs. Work from right to left or from top to bottom. Loop the thread under the needle and pull the needle gently to form a rounded stitch. Repeat stitches, inserting needle exactly where the thread came out inside the previous loop. When filling in with chain stitch, work several rows side by side and always in the same direction.

Lazy Daisy is a decorative stitch derived from the chain. Each loop is placed individually around a small circle to form a daisy with five or six petals. Practice making these little flowers in all sizes. Lazy Daisies should be done freehand.

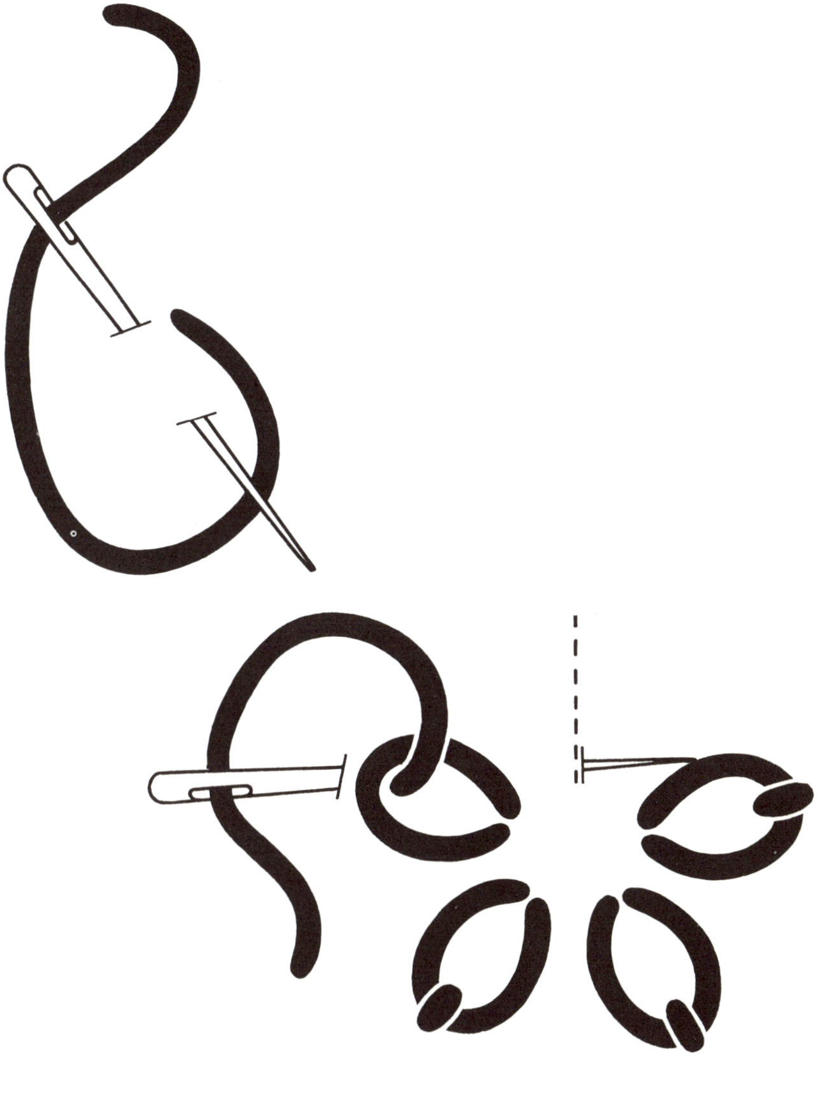

French Knot is a little bump stitch that is very useful in decorative embroidery. Bring threaded needle out at precisely the point you wish to place the knot. Hold needle with your left hand with the point toward yourself. Hold the part of the thread closest to the fabric in your right hand and twist it over the needle in an "over and under" motion. Do not release the thread. Hold it firmly in your right hand as you move the needle in an almost upright position, placing the point as close as possible to the original point of exit. Pull the needle through very carefully and release the thread at the very end. French Knots require a little practice but they are well worth the effort.

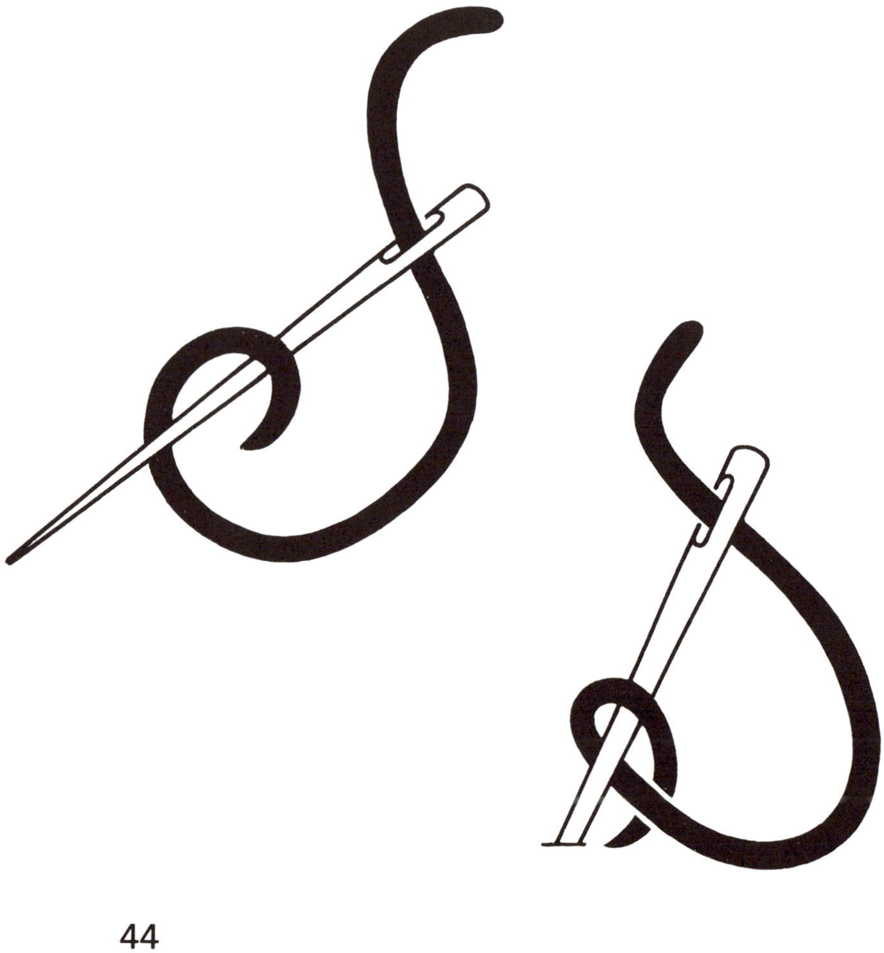

Herringbone can be used for edging or for decorative multicolored stripes.

The stitches used in this book are simple and easy to learn. Once you master them, you will be able to do some very attractive needlepoint without being a great expert.

PATTERNS

Enlarging a Pattern

To enlarge a pattern, trace it first on a sheet of tracing paper. Draw four lines around it to establish a margin and a definite size. Fold the paper in half, then in quarters and in eighths. Make sure the creases are sharp. Now take a paper large enough to accommodate the projected enlargement and fold it in as many squares as the smaller paper. Open flat and number the squares in consecutive order. Number them exactly the same way on both sheets of paper. If the paper does not lie flat, iron it with a warm iron. Copy the design one square at a time.

A much simpler and far more accurate way to enlarge (or reduce) a pattern is to have a Photostat copy made. Several small designs may be enlarged at one time on a Photostat and used as needed.

Tracing a Pattern

Transfer your design to sheer tracing paper. Tack the smoothly ironed fabric to a board with push pins or tacks. This prevents it from shifting. Place transfer paper shiny side down on the fabric and position your design on top of it. Pin both papers to the fabric and trace design carefully with a soft pencil. Don't use sharp metal points. Test the transfer paper before using. Some transfer paper is not of good quality and it is wise to find this out before completing your design. (If the fabric will not take a transfer [blankets, sweatshirts, loose knits, etc.], pin the design to the given fabric and outline the pattern with machine stitching or tiny hand stitches.) Press the paper with a very warm iron. The paper will become brittle and may be pulled away easily from the fabric.

Another way is to transfer your design on a very sheer fabric, then place this fabric on the underside of your work, pin in place and sew the outline of the pattern with small running stitches through both fabrics. The tiny stitches will indicate your design on the face of your fabric. Overembroider and leave the sheer fabric. This is a good method for transferring designs on sweaters. Don't use contrasting colors for your fine stitches. If they blend with your fabric, there will be no need to pick them out when the work is finished.

Select designs that are simple to outline (coloring book type). You can always make them more elaborate with extra stitches or bright colors.

MAKING A SMALL RUG

Use a standard size camp blanket, dark gray or navy. Cut in half and line up edges very neatly. Pin together, and using a yard stick and a piece of tailor's chalk, draw a series of lines at 2-inch intervals across the blanket. Work a tiny running stitch through both thicknesses following these lines. Use a fine wool or acrylic yarn of matching color. Do not remove stitches after finishing rug.

To transfer the cat design illustrated, first enlarge the pattern to 30 x 16 (each square will measure 2 inches). Trace the design onto a sheet of fine tracing paper and pin this to the blanket. It is not possible to transfer designs with transfer paper on a heavy wool fabric. Simply stitch the tracing paper on the blanket with small Running stitches. Work the entire cat design with these stitches. Now, run a very warm iron over the paper. This makes the paper brittle and easy to tear away. The cat is then worked in an outline stitch with medium weight wool rug yarn in a light color. The mouse, eyelids, and

tongue of the cat are worked in pink yarn, filling in the entire area with Stem stitches. Work as much as possible through both thicknesses of blanket. Outline with Half Diamond or Herringbone stitch. Rug may be oval, round or rectangular.

For stitches used in this project, see pages 21, 32, 40, 41.

Small rug made out
of an army blanket.

Close-up showing stem stitches filling in cat's eyelids and tongue and the mouse.

MAKING BUTTONS AND JEWELRY

Buttons and jewelry are fun to make and cost only a few pennies. Findings for making buttons are available at notion counters in most stores. Instructions are included and are easy to follow. The button is like a little metal box. The piece of embroidered fabric is smoothed over the top part of the box and tucked under. The bottom part of the box snaps into place and holds the fabric tightly.

The tiny elephant on the bottom right of the photograph on page 57 was worked on a scrap of #20 petit point canvas with two strands of yarn. Copy this and the other designs shown or make your own. Bits of embroidery from old handkerchiefs or blouses may be cut out and used to cover buttons. If fabric is too thin, place a bit of lining under it. To save time on needlepoint buttons, tint the background and work the design only.

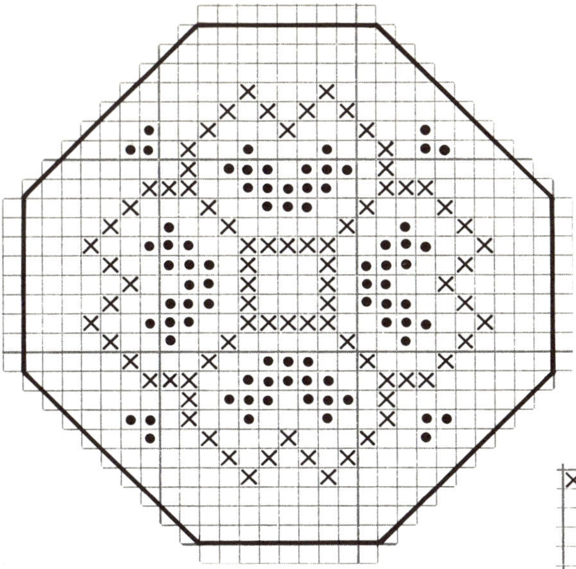

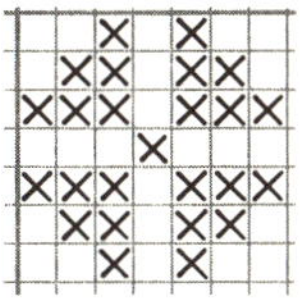

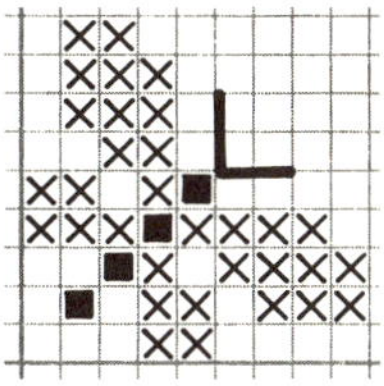

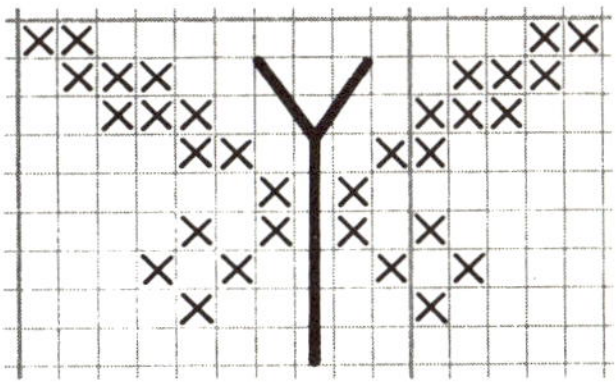

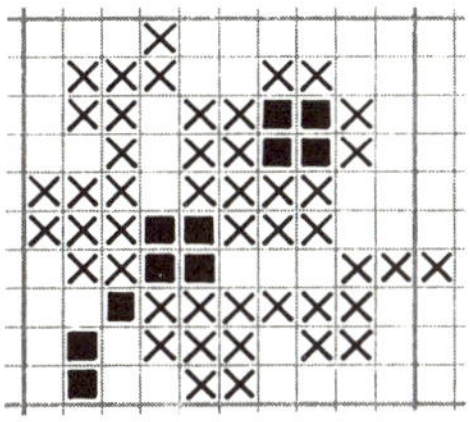

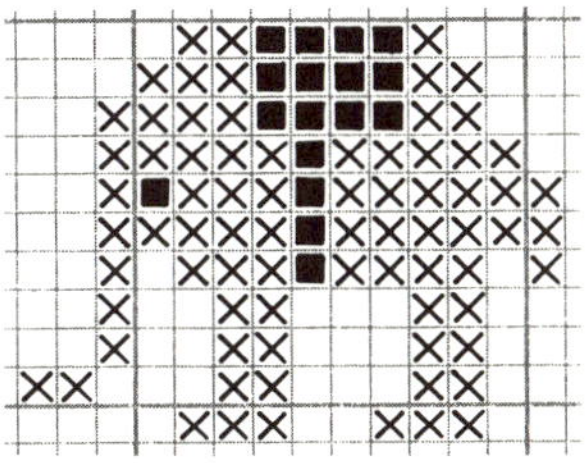

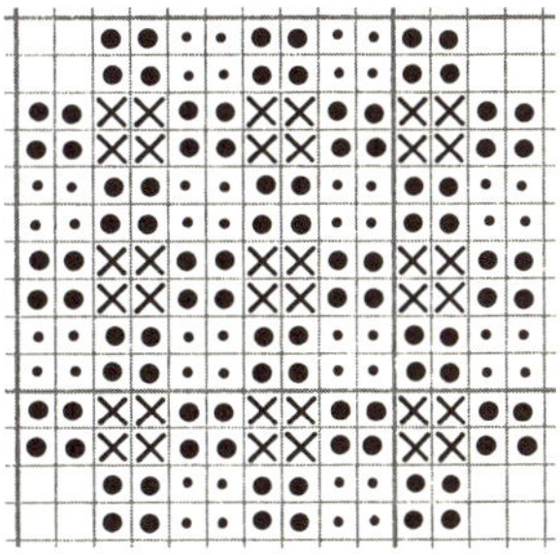

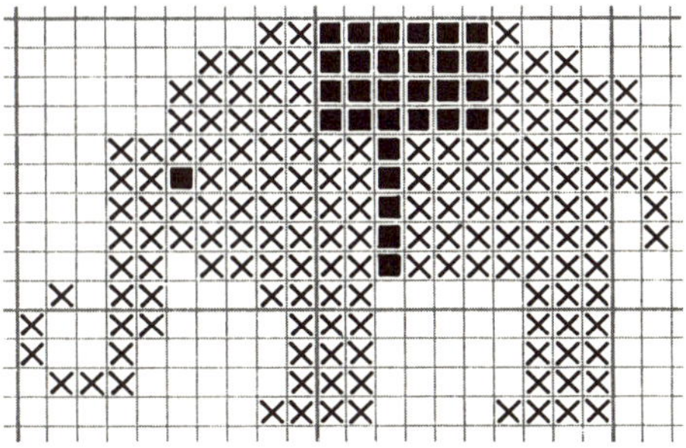

Design for jewelry and buttons on plain fabric

Needlepoint jewelry can be worked on canvas or other fabric with any thread. In the photograph, the owl is embroidered on burlap with scraps of bright yarn in the Chain and Stem stitches with French Knots for eyes. Draw a circle around a water glass rim and follow outline with Chain stitch. Leave ¼-inch margin. Cut a piece of cardboard the same size as the circle drawn on the burlap. Glue cardboard to the back of the burlap within embroidered circle with white all-purpose glue. Fold extra fabric over cardboard and glue again. Let dry,

A variety of button and jewelry designs.

trim rough edges and fasten a pin finding to the back of the pin. Jewelry findings are sold in craft supply stores.

The pin on the left of the photograph is worked in Half Cross stitches on #10 canvas in a dark blue background and bright colors. The same pattern worked in a larger Smyrna Cross on a larger square of canvas will make a very attractive buckle. Several patterns in bright colors will look marvelous on a handbag.

To make the buckle illustrated, fold back open raw edges

of canvas cut to the desired size and finish all around with Single Overcast stitch. Line buckle with a piece of cotton or burlap. Cut this half an inch larger than the buckle, place it on the wrong side, fold all excess under and pin wrong sides together. Check right side to make sure that the lining does not show and sew firmly in place with small stitches. Attach to belt by sewing it to one end and use large hooks and eyes on the other end.

For stitches used in these projects, see pages 15, 16, 41, 42, 44.

Single Overcast

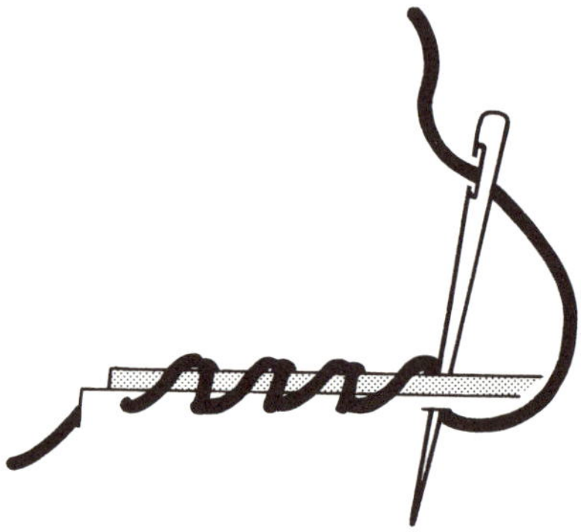

Double Overcast

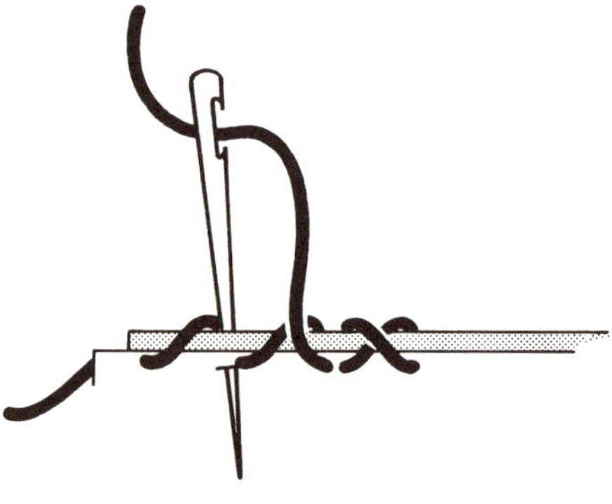

Cross Overcast

Buckle worked in Open Diamond on #3½ canvas with wood beads placed in centers.

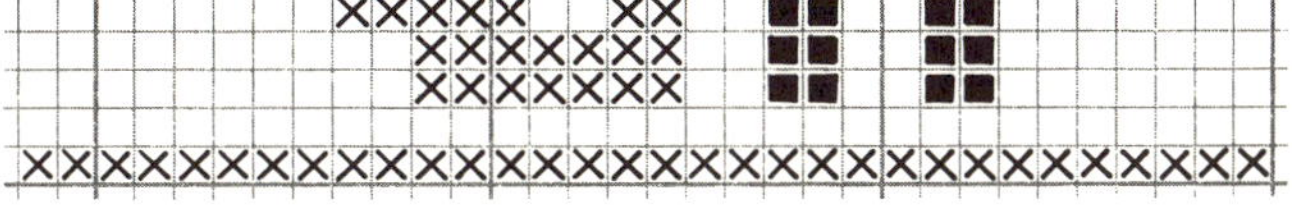

Pre-Columbian design idea for a buckle.

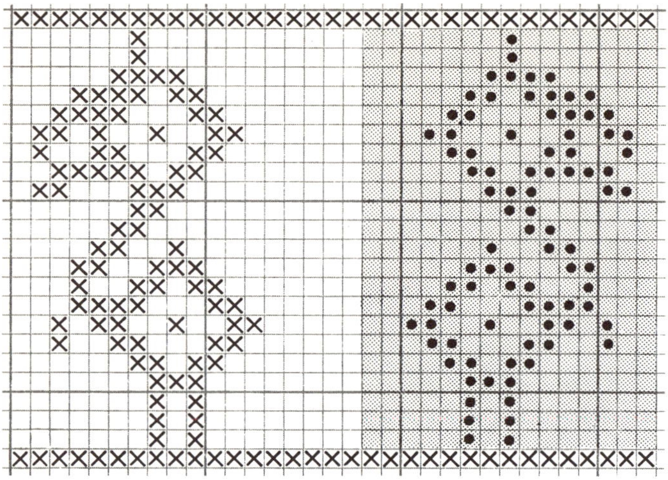

Pre-Columbian design idea for a buckle.

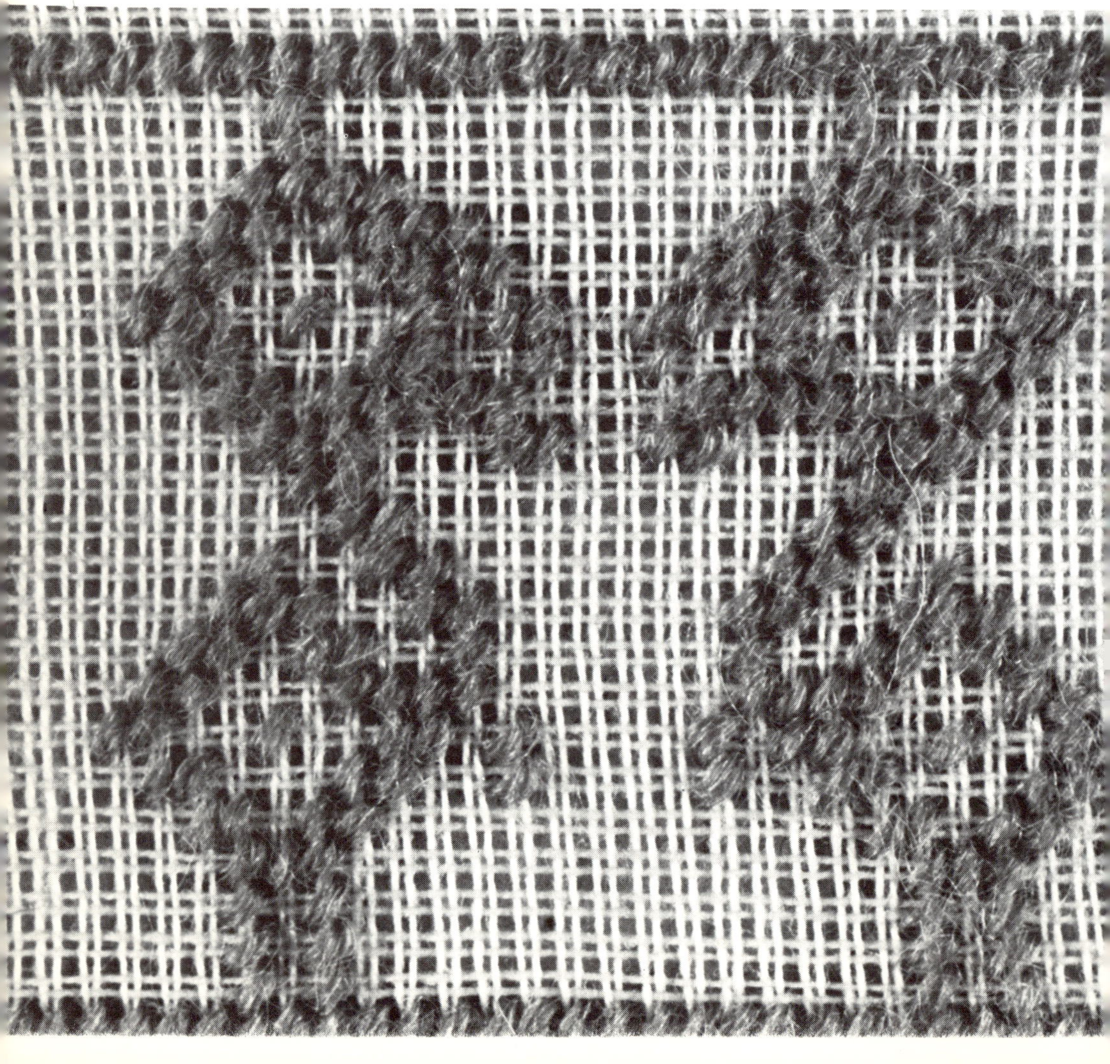

MAKING A DIRECTOR'S CHAIR

Remove existing seat and back, open all seams and cut two pieces of canvas for each. Use heavy #3½ or #4 canvas and work with string or macramé cord. Allow an excess margin of 1½ inch all around. Fold this margin *in,* top and bottom, so that the raw edges of the canvas are on the inside and between the layers of canvas and baste. Begin by working the top edge with a Double Overcast stitch. The chair shown was worked with the Open Diamond stitch in navy jute cord. Work through both thicknesses of canvas, pulling the cord tightly as you go. The top and bottom lines will be worked through four layers of canvas as the edges are folded in. Finish the bottom line with a Double Overcast stitch. The sides are left unfinished since they get tucked in and folded under, when chair seat and back are replaced on the frame. The back should be lined. This type of needlework is suitable for any chair that has a canvas or mesh cover.

For stitches used in this project, see pages 32, 58.

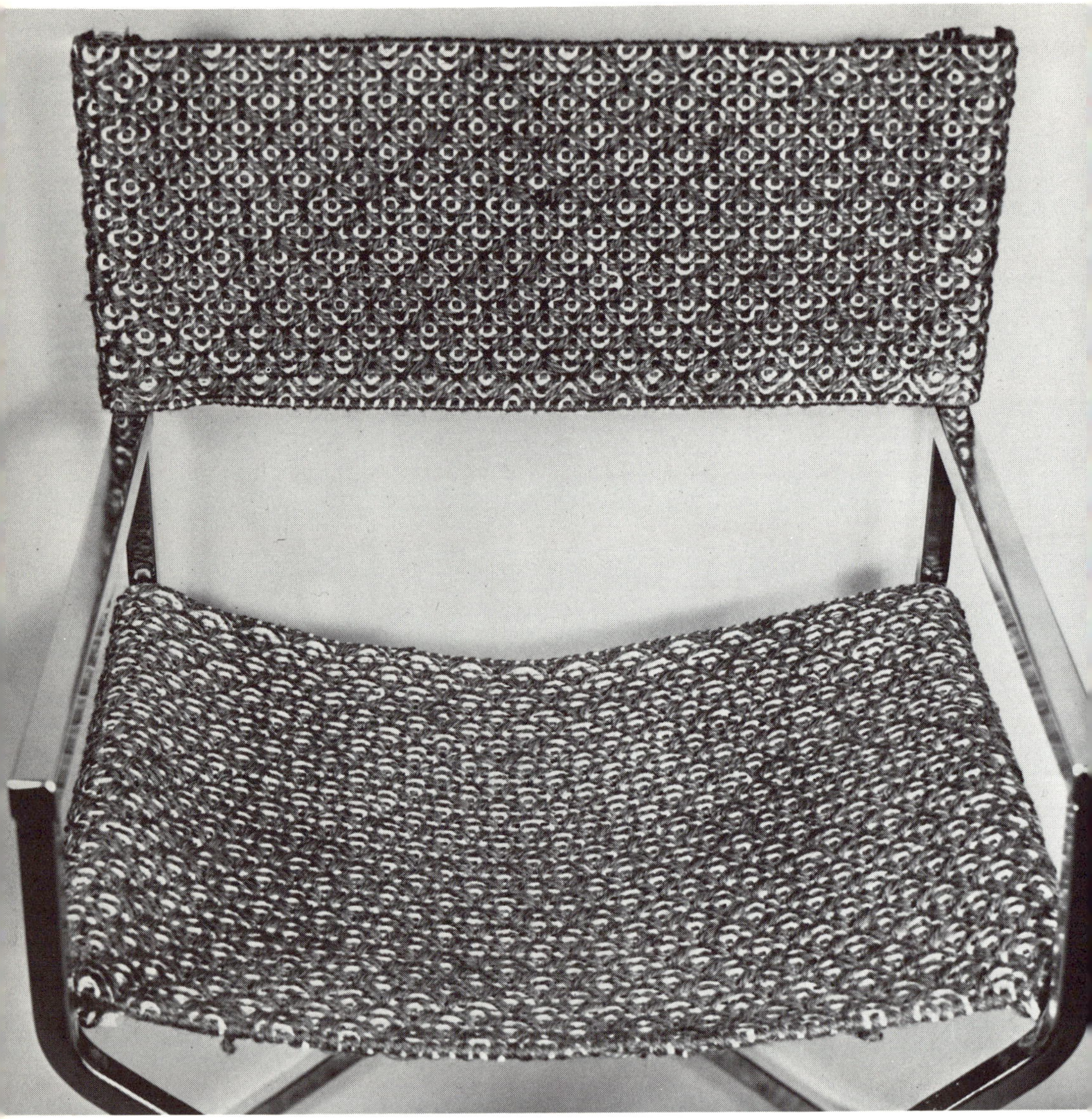

Director's Chair worked in Open Diamond in navy jute cord.

MAKING A BELT

Measure the length to fit your waist, allowing at least 3 inches at each end for folding over a buckle. It is important to leave extra canvas at the end even if you have to cut it off later. Sometimes the canvas will pull tightly and "shrink" a little or the bulk of the stitches will make the belt a little shorter. It is not advisable to piece a belt, so allow extra canvas before you begin.

Allow twice as much canvas for the width of the belt. Fold over so that both raw edges meet in the center in the back. Check the number of stitches you will need for the pattern. Work the first few stitches of each line to establish the pattern, if necessary. The canvas should not overlap in the back of the belt. Work through the two thicknesses of canvas at all times. Leave top and bottom lines for a Single or Double

Four belt designs. From top, Herringbone stitch in two colors worked on #3½ canvas in rattail cord; Herringbone worked with four colors in sisal gift wrap on #3½ inch canvas; Herringbone, open stitches with canvas showing through worked in heavy jute packing cord

on #3½ inch canvas; Chevron stitch with canvas showing as part of the textured design, worked in blue macra-cord on white #4 canvas (also shown in color).

Overcast stitch. When using heavy string or macramé cord, allow canvas to show through as part of the pattern. A double thickness of canvas is very durable. When belt is finished, measure again, attach buckles or tie strings and cut off excess. Use a two-part buckle rather than the one piece. Although handsome, these belts are very bulky and should not overlap. Tuck in ends on the wrong side very carefully. There is no need to line belts. Linings add extra bulk and it is much easier to repair a belt that is not lined.

For stitches used in this project, see pages 21, 28, 58.

MAKING A WINDOW SHADE

This project was worked on #6 single mesh canvas tinted brown with indelible marking pen. Linen rug warp was used but any soft string would be adequate. It is important to have a clean look without knots and tail ends on the back. Measure the length of the shade and use a length of string three times longer. Begin at lower right and using the Chevron stitch, work in a vertical line going up. Cross over at the top and work down with the same length of string. Allow a 6-inch tassel at the beginning and you should have 6 inches left at the finish. Tie them together. If the strand is not long enough to cover two lines plus the fringe, use a longer strand. Once you know the length of the string, precut all of them. To obtain a random fringe, cut some of the strands a little longer. Work the first and last line as well as the top and bottom through two thicknesses of canvas by folding over the edges. Tie fringes with tight knots. Add beads if desired. Fold top over a wood dowel or curtain rod.

For stitch used in this project, see page 28.

Window shade worked in a wide Chevron stitch in linen rug warp on #6 single mesh canvas.

Window shade closeup.

MAKING A HANDBAG

Select a pattern and the fabric on which it will be worked. Determine the size and cut a pattern from a sheet of newspaper. Illustrated are outlines for three basic shapes of handbags you can easily make yourself without professional experience.

Whatever style you choose, it is easier to work on one piece of fabric. When working on heavy canvas, the less cutting and piecing, the better. In the style at bottom, the base is part of the body of the handbag and you must allow for it when you measure the fabric. The gussets are inserted at the sides only.

Prepare fabric by edging all around with tape or machine stitching to prevent fraying. Allow at least 1 inch border all

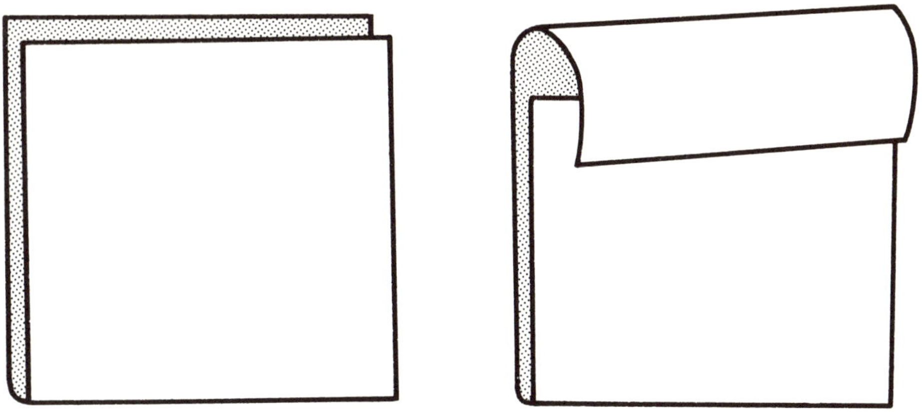

Three basic shapes for handbags: at top, folded in half and with flap; at bottom, with gusset.

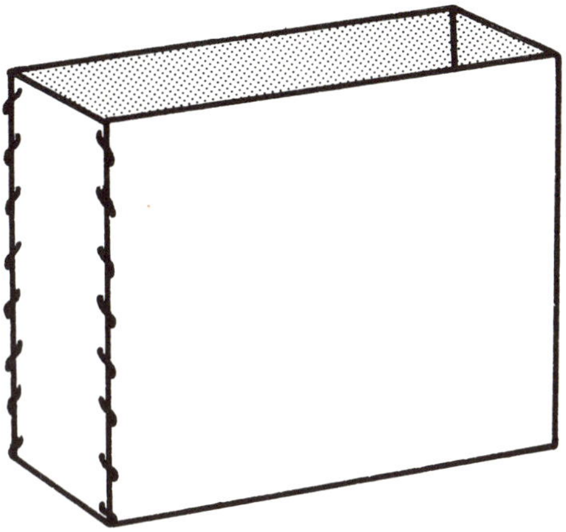

around. Needlepoint canvas should be folded over at top and bottom and the first and last lines worked through both thicknesses of the canvas. This creates a smoothly finished edge that stays in shape. Work the needlepoint over the entire fabric. Tuck in all tail ends and don't leave any knots. If you

work with heavy string or macramé, leave very long ends that may be worked under the stitches on the wrong side of the work. For this, a crochet hook is very handy.

When needlepoint is finished, cut a lining the same size as the fabric for the handbag. Be sure the lining is heavy enough to cover the stitches. Light cotton will not do as lining for a bag worked with string. If the stitches are very bumpy, use an interlining of felt or some other thick fabric. Place finished needlepoint on a flat surface wrong side up. If it is embroidered fabric, press it. Press lining. If using interlining, place it over the needlepoint and baste with large stitches catching the underside of the handbag very lightly. Place lining over the interlining right side up. Line up the edges and pin in place. Lining has to be pinned in very smoothly or it will bag later. Fold in edge of needlepoint to meet folded edge of lining and baste all around. Remove pins. Now fold lined bag in the desired shape and close the sides with any Overcast stitch (see page 58). Using the same stitch, finish all the edges with matching or contrasting yarns. Gusset insert must be prepared separately, lined and then basted to the body of the handbag and finished with Overcast stitches.

These instructions are given primarily for finishing handbags worked with heavy string or macramé cord. These are difficult to machine stitch and turn inside out. They must be worked on the right side and finished by hand. For handles, use a length of chain purchased in a hardware store or braid some leftover matching yarn. Attach handles directly to side of bag with needle and thread or loop through a wooden or plastic curtain ring and sew the curtain ring to the handbag. Pin handles and try them out for length and ease of handling before sewing permanently.

Nearly all the design ideas in the book are suitable for handbags. All are quick and easy to do. Some can be finished in two or three hours. The burlap and string handbag shown is one example. It requires one half yard of burlap, a ball of

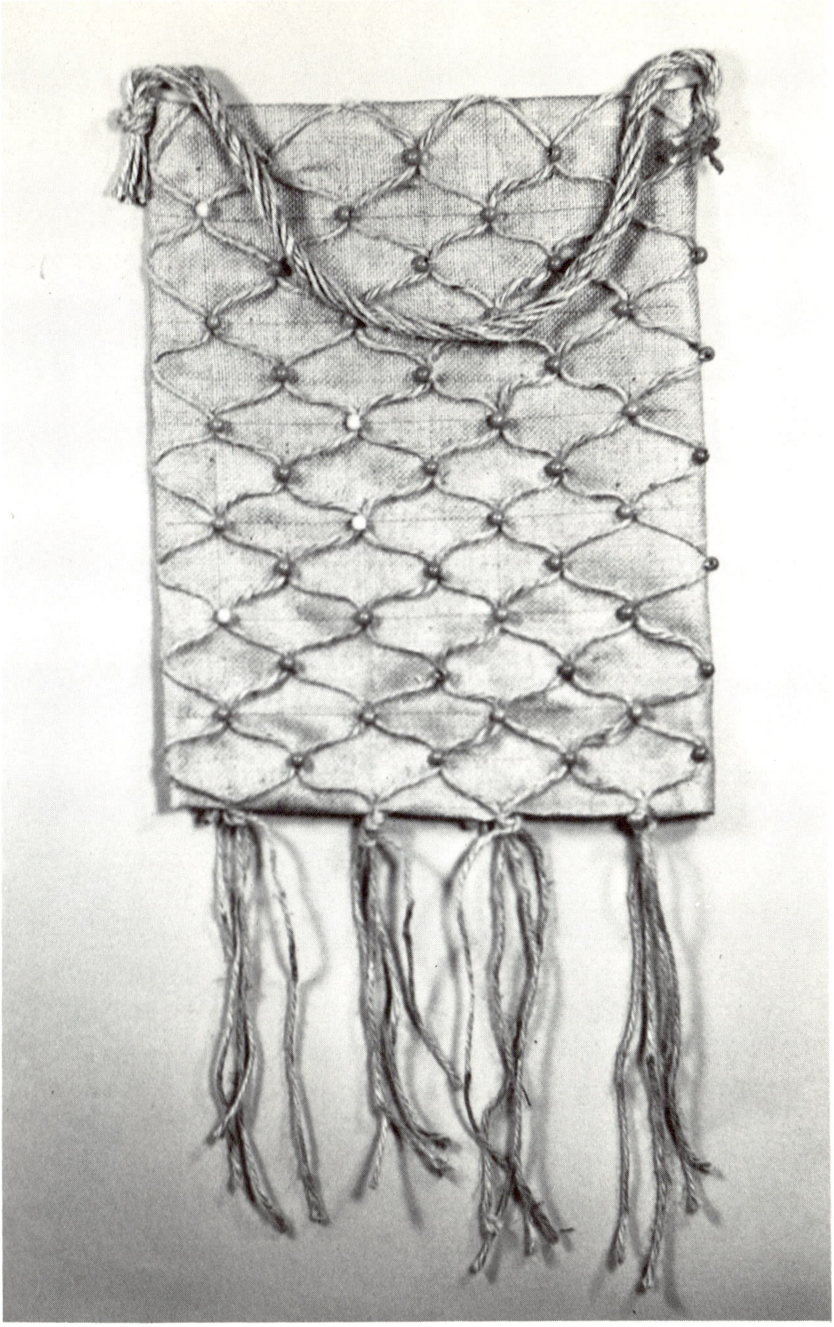

Burlap and string bag.

heavy jute twine and 120 macramé beads with large holes. The burlap is folded in half and a pencil line drawn on the fold. Working from the outer edge toward the fold line, take large surface stitches on the burlap (see diagram). The string is premeasured in 50-inch lengths. As each line is finished, the remainder of string is left uncut. Both sides of the handbag are worked the same way. The stitches are straight but the weight of the string makes them curve a little, forming the rounded trellis effect.

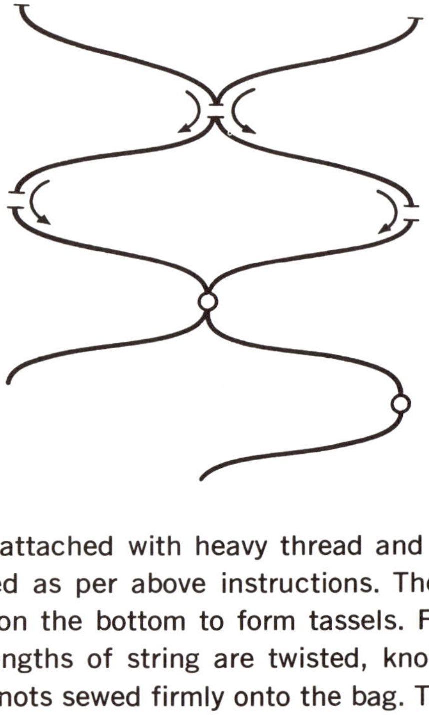

Beads are attached with heavy thread and the bag finished and lined as per above instructions. The strings are tied together on the bottom to form tassels. For a handle, ten 20-inch lengths of string are twisted, knotted at each end and the knots sewed firmly onto the bag. To achieve an even geometric outline, divide the burlap into 2-inch squares. Draw lines with chalk pencil.

Handbag and belt set, worked in linen rug warp on #6 single mesh canvas in a narrow Chevron stitch. The belt is striped with red navy cord, which is the same weight as the rug warp, but a little shinier.

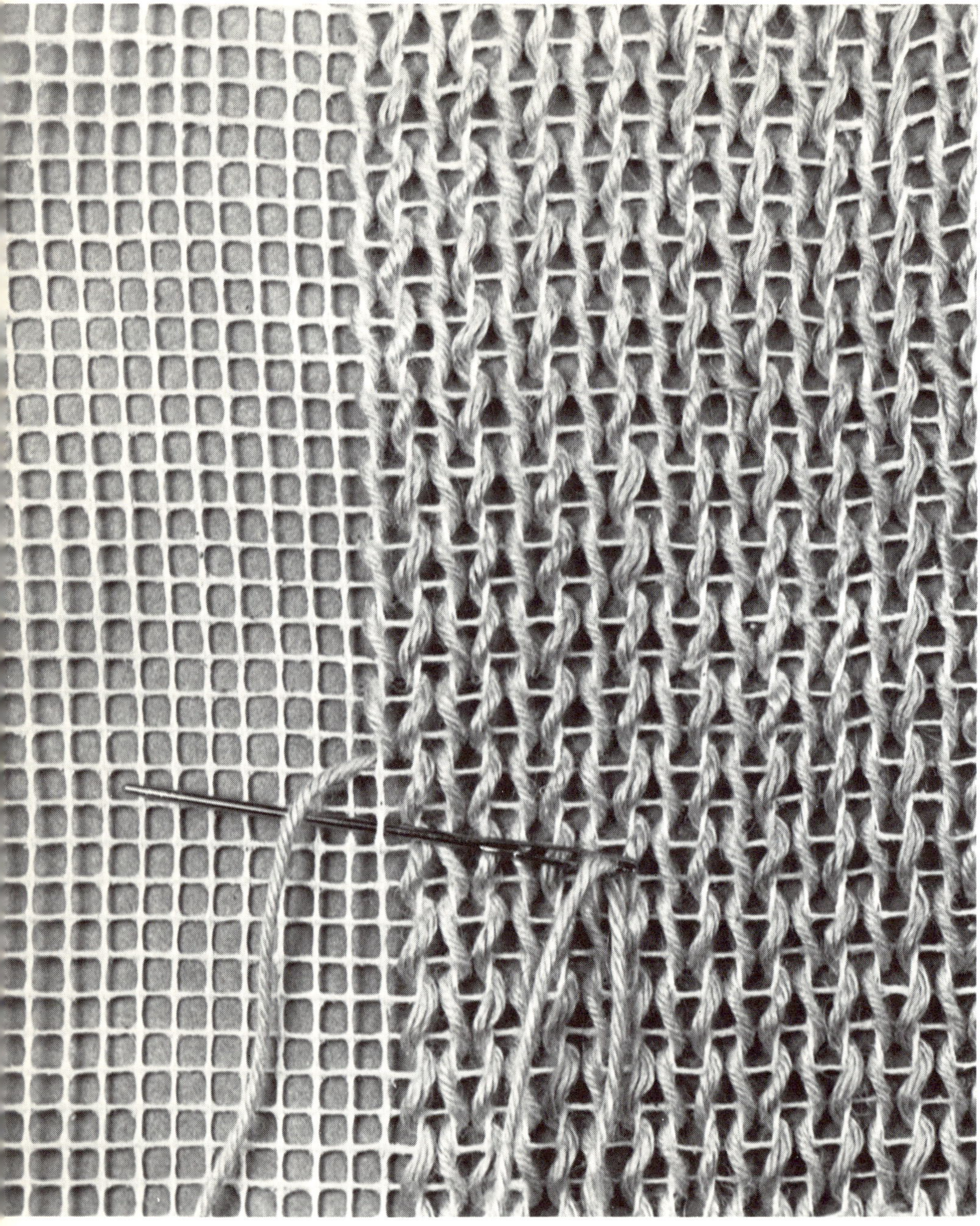

Handbag closeup

MAKING A FRAME

Draw a rectangle 16 x 18 and outline with Chain stitches. Allow a 3-inch margin. Draw center outline to fit mirror or picture and work with Chain stitches. Cover the entire surface with Lazy Daisies worked freehand and overlapping slightly. The picture frame shown was worked with raffia on burlap.

When finished, cut a piece of plywood to fit the frame, place needlework on top and check fit. Cut the center from fabric, allowing 1 inch for folding under. Mark outline on plywood and glue a small mirror or picture in place. Fold back the raw edges of fabric around the center opening. Clip corner to square and tack with tiny stitches. Place the entire needlework over the plywood. Position the center opening over the mirror. Place a few thumb tacks all around to prevent it from shifting. Turn over and staple the excess fabric to the back of the plywood. Turn corners carefully. Glue a piece of felt to the back to cover rough edges. Remove thumb tacks.

For stitches used in this project, see pages 42–43.

Sunglass cases: Top right, a slanted Chevron stitch as indicated in upper left sample of canvas. Worked in washable acrylic yarn on #6 single mesh canvas. Top left, single Herringbone as indicated in lower right of canvas sample worked in raffia on #6 single mesh (also shown in color).

MAKING SUNGLASS CASES

Since sunglasses vary in size, it is not possible to give general measurements. Draw a rectangle on paper to accommodate glasses. Allow 1/4-inch margin all around and cut a strip of canvas the same width but twice the length of pattern. Cut a piece of lining the same size. Work needlepoint to within the margin and fold in half, right side out. Tuck in side margins and finish with Overcast stitch.

Fold lining in half wrong side out and stitch firmly at sides. Slip lining into canvas case. Press in corners with a pencil. Finish opening at top by folding raw edges of canvas and lining against each other and working a neat Overcast stitch all around, picking up both fabrics as you go.

Lazy Daisy Frame (also shown in color).

DESIGNS FOR OVEREMBROIDERING A DENIM JACKET

Enlarge the design so that the squares measure one square inch. Transfer it onto the back of a jacket (if jacket is washable, wash and dry first). Embroider jacket with Chain stitches in crewel yarn on sun and bird and Stem stitches on the rest of the design. Fill in the outlines with rows of Stem stitches or little straight lines. The mushroom is filled with tiny Cross stitches. The front of the jacket is worked with Cross stitches, and sequins are placed inside the diamonds under the pockets. Some sequins are sprinkled on the main design. Use bright colors in any washable yarns. Avoid using large open stitches because they have a tendency to catch.

See also color photograph.

Lee

Embroidery design for denim jacket

DESIGN FOR OVEREMBROIDERING A BLANKET

With a yardstick and tailor's chalk, mark off a standard size navy blanket with an all-over diamond pattern (see color photograph). Follow the lines with Chain stitch using machine-washable acrylic yarn or whatever colorfast yarn you happen to have. Trace suggested center design illustrated as per instructions for cat and mouse rug on page 52, or make your own free-form design. Draw it with chalk and follow outlines with yarn. Keep wrong side of work as neat as possible. Edge blanket with a Simple Overcast or Herringbone stitch.

A solid-color coverlet may be embroidered much the same way or a printed one overembroidered with matching yarns. If the coverlet is washable, be sure to use washable yarns.

Center design for blanket

DESIGN FOR OVEREMBROIDERING A BLANKET

Freehand simple embroidery on jeans, handbag and belt. Draw a snaky line freehand and overembroider in Chain or Stem stitch. Place single Chain stitch loops on either side of this line in a carefree fashion. The handbag and jeans are bought ready-made and overembroidered. The belt is made of burlap but may be made in any strong fabric.

OVEREMBROIDERING PRINTED FABRICS

The photographs show samples of overembroidered printed fabrics. Choose a simple print, and using Chain, Stem or Herringbone stitches, overembroider the print with matching or contrasting crewel yarn. There is no need to overembroider the entire print. If a large piece of fabric is overembroidered to be used for a skirt or jacket, be careful to overembroider all the repeat patterns the same way. Overembroidering is a very inexpensive way to lend a custom boutique look to ordinary fabrics. Use basic stitches, keep them small, and if the fabric is going to be washed, be sure to use washable threads and yarns.

For stitches used in all overembroidery projects, see pages 40–45.

Printed fabric overembroidered with Chain stitch.

OVEREMBROIDERING PRINTED FABRICS

Part of a printed fabric, overembroidered in Chain, Lazy Daisy and Stem stitches (also shown in color).

Ticking print overembroidered with Herringbone stitch in crayon colors (also shown in color).

A simple outline drawing of acrobats, worked in Chain stitch, suitable for a t-shirt or sweat shirt. This may be enlarged on heavy fabric and worked in bulky yarn for a wall hanging.

The transfers reproduced here are actual size. The designs may be used individually on ties, buttons, pockets, handbags, eyeglass cases, place mats and articles of clothing.

A pair of jeans embroidered with a number of little designs in washable cotton thread.

Butterfly design worked in heavy Yarn-Tys using the Stem stitch. The design was traced on an 18×18 piece of Knot-on fabric, though any bulky fabric will do, and then outlined, beginning with the outer line and working toward the center. This design may be worked with thinner yarns on a smaller, finer fabric (also shown in color).

List of Suppliers

Retail and mail order:

George Wells
The Ruggery
565 Cedar Swamp Road
Glen Head, N.Y. 11545
Undyed wool yarns, dyes, dyeing instructions, cotton backing, burlap, needles, transfer pencils and fabric slitters

Wholesale distributors:

East House
15 East 22 Street
New York, N.Y. 10010
Yarn-Tys and colored twine

Reynolds Yarns, Inc.
220 Fifth Avenue
New York, N.Y. 10001
Machine-washable acrylic yarns and canvas

Lilly Mills Co.
P.O. Box 88
Shelby, N.C. 28150
Macramé materials and canvas

Paternayan Bros., Inc.
312 East 95 Street
New York, N.Y. 10028
Persian yarn, Rya cloth and canvas

Write to wholesale distributors for a list of retail stores nearest you.